Ding Dong Dead

Adapted by
Mawby Green
and
Ed Feilbert

From *Double Jeu* by
Robert Thomas

A Samuel French Acting Edition

New York Hollywood London Toronto
SAMUELFRENCH.COM

Copyright © 1979, 1986 by Eric Mawby Green and Edward Allen Feilbert

ALL RIGHTS RESERVED

CAUTION: Professionals and amateurs are hereby warned that *DING DONG DEAD* is subject to a Licensing Fee. It is fully protected under the copyright laws of the United States of America, the British Commonwealth, including Canada, and all other countries of the Copyright Union. All rights, including professional, amateur, motion picture, recitation, lecturing, public reading, radio broadcasting, television and the rights of translation into foreign languages are strictly reserved. In its present form the play is dedicated to the reading public only.

The amateur live stage performance rights to *DING DONG DEAD* are controlled exclusively by Samuel French, Inc., and licensing arrangements and performance licenses must be secured well in advance of presentation. PLEASE NOTE that amateur Licensing Fees are set upon application in accordance with your producing circumstances. When applying for a licensing quotation and a performance license please give us the number of performances intended, dates of production, your seating capacity and admission fee. Licensing Fees are payable one week before the opening performance of the play to Samuel French, Inc., at 45 W. 25th Street, New York, NY 10010.

Licensing Fee of the required amount must be paid whether the play is presented for charity or gain and whether or not admission is charged.

Stock licensing fees quoted upon application to Samuel French, Inc.

For all other rights than those stipulated above, apply to: Samuel French, Inc.

Particular emphasis is laid on the question of amateur or professional readings, permission and terms for which must be secured in writing from Samuel French, Inc.

Copying from this book in whole or in part is strictly forbidden by law, and the right of performance is not transferable.

Whenever the play is produced the following notice must appear on all programs, printing and advertising for the play: "Produced by special arrangement with Samuel French, Inc."

Due authorship credit must be given on all programs, printing and advertising for the play.

No one shall commit or authorize any act or omission by which the copyright of, or the right to copyright, this play may be impaired.
No one shall make any changes in this play for the purpose of production.
Publication of this play does not imply availability for performance. Both amateurs and professionals considering a production are strongly advised in their own interests to apply to Samuel French, Inc., for written permission before starting rehearsals, advertising, or booking a theatre.
No part of this book may be reproduced, stored in a retrieval system, or transmitted in any form, by any means, now known or yet to be invented, including mechanical, electronic, photocopying, recording, videotaping, or otherwise, without the prior written permission of the publisher.

ISBN 978-0-573-61996-0   Printed in U.S.A.   #6140

CHARACTERS

Louise
Monique
Rudy
Corbeau
Michel
Inspector Murzeau
1st Policeman
2nd Policeman

(Rudy and Michel are played by the same actor.)

The action takes place in the living room of a lonely house in the Chevreuse Valley, France.

ACT ONE

Scene 1: A morning in April.
Scene 2: The following morning.
Scene 3: One hour later.

ACT TWO

Scene 1: One hour later.
Scene 2: One hour later.

Ding Dong Dead

ACT ONE

Scene 1

The rather luxurious living room of a lovely house in the Chevreuse Valley, France.

U.C. *is a large bay window, with French doors opening on to the terrace. The woods beyond are dark and silent.* U.R. *is a staircase to the bedrooms.* U.L. *is a hall to the main entrance and a door to the kitchen. The furnishings are a mixture of modern and antique, rather chic and baroque: large sofa, armchairs, desk, bar, etc.*

It is spring of this year. The curtains are drawn. The room is in semi-darkness. LOUISE, the maid, enters from the kitchen. She draws the window curtains. Sunshine floods the room. LOUISE opens the French doors and breathes in the fresh air. She then looks at her watch and puts the breakfast tray on a table near the sofa. Finally, she goes to the telephone on the desk and presses the intercom button.

LOUISE. (*pleasantly*) Hello? Good morning, madame! It's nine o'clock! . . . I hope I didn't wake you? . . . Then why didn't you ring for me, madame? . . . (*cooing in sympathy*) Oh, you slept badly. What a pity! Oh! . . . Oh, madame, I suspected monsieur hadn't come home last night, when I didn't see his car in the driveway . . . But, madame, why think he was out gambling again? Perhaps he had a late supper with friends and they persuaded him to sleep over! . . . Come down to breakfast, you'll feel better! I tried to make the croissants exactly as you like them! . . . Good! I'll just go down to the gate to see if the mail has arrived.

(*She hangs up, sighs, and goes out by the terrace. The room is empty for a few seconds. A bedroom door is heard closing. MONIQUE appears and comes down the staircase. There is a sweetness about this very pretty woman. The dress she is wearing is simple but expensive and in very good taste. Tired and nervous, she sits on the sofa, stares at her black coffee, drinks it, then tries to eat something but can't. She pushes the tray away. LOUISE, who has returned, watches her for a moment before going over with a bundle of letters, newspapers and magazines.*)

LOUISE. (*continued*) Here is the mail, madame . . . (*MONIQUE starts looking through the mail.*)
MONIQUE. Bills, bills . . . a summons . . . bills! (*Suddenly, she puts her head in her hands . . . her nerves crack.*) I can't go on like this any longer! I can't! Each day Rudy behaves worse than the day before! . . . Louise, you've been in service in this house for a year now, working for my husband. Has he always been like this?
LOUISE. (*embarrassed*) Well . . . madame . . .
MONIQUE. A drinker? A gambler?
LOUISE. Yes . . . and no!
MONIQUE. I don't understand.
LOUISE. Whenever monsieur had money, he liked to go out drinking and gambling. But when there was a drought, he had to stay at home, of course. This peaceful valley was like medicine to him! Well . . . (*She laughs but immediately rues it.*) Well, you see, since he

married madame . . . a woman of means . . . the situation, unfortunately, has been aggravated.

MONIQUE. I always refuse him money! For his own good!

LOUISE. Yes, but you always give it to him in the end! To his detriment!

MONIQUE. (*with tears in her eyes*) I know. But I love him, Louise! . . . He was so different when we first met! How he has changed in . . . three months!

LOUISE. Ah, madame, I can still picture you arriving here, smiling and happy, after the honeymoon. Monsieur had sent word to get the house in order . . . You had wanted to get married in Geneva?

MONIQUE. Yes, I was born in Switzerland.

LOUISE. And all your family is there?

MONIQUE. Family? One uncle, who never had time for me! He was always travelling!

LOUISE. Have you always been alone, madame?

MONIQUE. Yes . . . and alone the years passed . . . then suddenly everything changed for me! My uncle died and I inherited his fortune. The cage was open! I was free! I knew nothing of *life* but I knew I wanted to *live*!

LOUISE. Oh! la! la! And in Zermatt, on a skiing holiday, you met monsieur!!

MONIQUE. Yes . . . Rudy was stopping at the same hotel. I fell for him on sight, he was so charming, so full of life. A few days later he confided in me, told me he was short of funds . . . and I settled his hotel bill! . . . That's how it happened. In the twinkling of an eye!

LOUISE. Oh, we women are all alike! Love makes fools of us all! (*suddenly*) Oh! You don't think Monsieur Rudy knew you had money in the bank when he met you?

MONIQUE. . . . At first, I asked myself that question,

then put it out of my mind! But, thank heaven, my lawyer, in drawing up the marriage contract, saw to it that everything I have remains mine. Rudy can't touch my money!

LOUISE. And a good thing, too, or madame would already be ruined!

MONIQUE. Yes, indeed. Because soon after our marriage, Rudy threw it in my face that he had investigated the extent of my wealth before proposing . . .

LOUISE. (*shocked*) Oh!

MONIQUE. Yes, it didn't take Rudy long to show his true colors! On our honeymoon, Rudy lost forty thousand francs, in one night, gambling . . . and paid with a bad check. To keep him out of prison, I made it good. The following night he was in an automobile collision . . . drunken driving. I paid the damages. There was a drug traffic incident. I paid and paid again . . . but what could I do? I wanted Rudy by my side. When we came here, to this isolated spot, away from people and temptation, I hoped he might become again the man I fell in love with. My dream lasted two weeks . . .

LOUISE. Oh, if I had your money, and Michel behaved towards me like that, I'd say, 'Michel'—

MONIQUE. (*interrupting*) Michel? Who's Michel?

LOUISE. (*blushing*) Oh! I . . . I have a friend. Michel. We're keeping company. I mean, sort of . . . He . . .

MONIQUE. (*amused by her embarrassment*) Don't blush, Louise. Your private life is your own. But you never go out!

LOUISE. Well . . . the situation is a bit . . . special.

MONIQUE. If you'd rather not tell me . . .

LOUISE. Well, since this is a morning for exchanging confidences, madame, I might as well tell you the truth. My friend is . . . abroad . . . in Nigeria. He's a construction worker . . . on a dam. I couldn't follow him out so I stay at home and wait for his return.

MONIQUE. (*smiling*) Are you in love?

LOUISE. Oh yes, madame!

MONIQUE. How nice! The first happy news to brighten my morning! (*MONIQUE smiles at her. LOUISE returns the smile. They heave a little sigh together. And another one.*)

LOUISE. Here I am prattling away, and your coffee's getting cold! I'll get a fresh pot! (*She goes into the kitchen with the coffee pot. MONIQUE sees the mail in front of her and continues to sort it.*)

MONIQUE. Bills . . . bills! (*Suddenly, one envelope attracts her attention. It surprises and puzzles her. She looks at the address, checks the postmark and stares hard at the large black seal on the back of the envelope.*) Well? What's this? (*LOUISE returns with the coffee pot.*) Louise . . .

LOUISE. Madame?

MONIQUE. There's a letter for you.

LOUISE. (*putting down the coffee pot*) Oh?

MONIQUE. It's from Fresnes. The prison in Fresnes. (*LOUISE is glued to the spot. The women look at each other.*)

LOUISE. The prison . . . in Fresnes?

MONIQUE. Yes, Louise. (*She crosses to her.*) . . . I suppose it's from your friend . . . in Nigeria . . . who's building a dam? (*She hands LOUISE the letter.*)

LOUISE. . . . Yes, it is. (*She clasps the letter to her breast. She is distraught.*) But Michel has never written to me here before! Why? Why did he do it? (*suddenly frightened*) Oh! Monsieur must never know about this letter!

MONIQUE. As I said before, your private life is no concern of ours.

LOUISE. . . . Because if monsieur ever found out I had

received a letter from the prison in Fresnes . . . !

MONIQUE. Rudy make a show of being against society. It would make him laugh! Perhaps we ought to let him see it.

LOUISE. (*crying out*) No! Oh, no! *No!*

MONIQUE. Oh? Why not?

LOUISE. Because monsieur knows my friend . . . but he doesn't know he writes to me. I mean, Michel always writes me care of 'General Delivery!'

MONIQUE. You mean my husband knows the prisoner but doesn't know you keep in touch with him?

LOUISE. Yes, that's right. Oh, please, don't say a word about this letter!

MONIQUE. You don't have to worry, Louise. (*pause*) Well? Read your letter.

LOUISE. Yes . . . yes, of course. (*She nervously tears open the envelope and takes out the letter. The envelope falls on the pouffe. As she reads, her face gradually lights up. She squeals, building to a crescendo of joy.*) Oh! Oh! Oh!

MONIQUE. What is it?

LOUISE. Michel is being released on parole!

MONIQUE. Are you happy?

LOUISE. Oh, yes! He wasn't due to get out until Christmas . . . but because of good behaviour, he'll be free tomorrow morning! (*suddenly in a panic*) Oh, please, madame . . . now more than ever . . . don't tell monsieur! I'll pack my bags and tonight, when he's asleep, I'll slip out of the house!

MONIQUE. What?

LOUISE. I'm afraid monsieur will try to stop me!

MONIQUE. Stop you? (*forcefully*) Really, Louise, what is this all about? Why should my husband want to stop you from leaving? Why should he care if your friend is getting out of prison and you want to go away with him?

Louise. (*not daring to explain*) It's because . . . I mean, my friend . . . he . . .

Monique. (*impatiently*) Who is he? Who *is* your friend?

Louise. No!

Monique. Tell me! Who is Michel?

(*The sound of a car screeching to a halt on the gravel driveway is heard. The car door slams. MONIQUE and LOUISE jump. LOUISE goes to the terrace to see who has arrived.*)

Louise. (*terrified*) It's monsieur! Please, I beg you, not a word about this letter!

(*She quickly exits to the kitchen, taking the letter with her. Suddenly, MONIQUE spots the envelope on the pouffe. Instinctively, she shoves it between two sofa cushions. She sits down at her breakfast tray quickly and acts as natural as possible. RUDY enters. He is handsome, with the charm of a scoundrel. He moves with grace and elegance, though this morning he is staggering from drink. His suit is beautifully tailored. A raincoat is thrown over his shoulders. His tie is undone and he is smoking a cigarillo. He comes to the center of the room.*)

Rudy. (*ironically*) Why, darling, up already?

Monique. (*calmly*) Why, darling, not yet in bed?

Rudy. (*laughing*) The perfect retort! Yes, that's why I married you, Monique! For your Parisian wit . . . and your Swiss francs!

MONIQUE. You have never been so honest!

RUDY. Because I have never been so drunk! I'm sloshed! (*And he adds:*) In vino veritas! (*He bends to kiss her. She pushes him away.*)

MONIQUE. You reek of whiskey! You smell like a pig!

RUDY. Pigs, my darling, rarely smell like whiskey! . . . Ah, coffee! (*He drinks.*) Before you know it, my dear, I'll be as fresh as a daisy!

MONIQUE. Can I ask you something?

RUDY. Of course. Anything at all.

MONIQUE. Where did you spend the night?

RUDY. At a club . . . gambling! (*slight pause*) Ah! Not a word of reproach! What a marvelous wife you are! Such a pity you have all those millions in the bank! You should have been poor. I would have loved you more. I might even have gone to work for you! What do you think of that?

MONIQUE. (*dryly*) I think that somehow it's all my fault. (*RUDY laughs.*)

RUDY. I won't argue. Now can I ask you something?

MONIQUE. Of course. Anything at all.

RUDY. Can you give me a check?

MONIQUE. I'll think about it.

RUDY. There isn't time. It's urgent. There's a man waiting outside in the car for his money. He escorted me home. People are so distrustful. You see, my darling, like the song says, 'I played and lost!' Where's your checkbook? (*He looks for it on the desk.*) Where is it? (*a long pause*) Have you gone deaf?

MONIQUE. No. I have regained my senses. I'm not giving you any more money.

RUDY. What? Now I've gone deaf! I didn't hear you!

MONIQUE. I'm not writing you another check. I reached that decision last night. (*RUDY bursts out laughing.*)

Rudy. You never cease to amuse me! (*suddenly, deadly serious*) Where is your checkbook?
Monique. I hid the checkbook. Don't force the drawer! You won't find it.
Rudy. (*turning ugly*) Don't-force-the-drawer! It doesn't pay to be nice, I can see that. Where is it?

(*He starts towards the bar. She tries to block his way. RUDY grabs MONIQUE by the wrist and hurls her across the room, where she stumbles over a piece of furniture. MONIQUE cries out. LOUISE rushes into the room.*)

Louise. (*alarmed*) No! Don't hit her! Please don't hit her!
Rudy. (*dryly*) Louise, mind your *own* business. Not mine. Do you understand?
Louise. (*turning pale*) Yes, monsieur . . .
Rudy. You know I always have my way. Don't you?
Louise. . . . Yes, monsieur. I know. (*a significant and explosive silence*)
Rudy. Good! There's a man in my car. Tell him to come in. And you can also tell him my wife is writing him a check.
Louise. Yes, monsieur. (*Subdued, she exits by the terrace. RUDY turns towards his wife, detaining her.*)
Rudy. . . . Because you are going to write it, my darling, aren't you? You're going to fetch your checkbook from its hiding place because it would be terribly embarrassing if an 'incident' were to take place in the presence of a guest. A painful incident. Painful for you, I mean. (*MONIQUE sits.*)
Monique. . . . Well! Today you've really dropped

your mask! How difficult it must have been to remain 'charming' for three months! What a farce!

RUDY. Yes, but what a profit!

MONIQUE. It's *my* money, safe in my Swiss bank. You won't get it!

RUDY. And you, a practising catholic! Saint Martin tore his cloak in two!

MONIQUE. . . . To cover a poor man! Not to support a gambler, a drunk, a cheat, liar, sadist . . . (*She fights back her tears.*)

RUDY. Finished?

MONIQUE. (*suddenly becoming firm and strong*) Rudy . . . I've reached a decision.

RUDY. Another one?

MONIQUE. I'm returning to Switzerland.

RUDY. (*mockingly*) You don't say!

MONIQUE. And file there for a divorce!

RUDY. Do you think I'd let you? Do you think I want to lose my dear little security girl? No, not after all the trouble I took to win you! Why, I'd rather strangle you . . . bury you at the bottom of the garden . . . and let the money come to me . . . in the normal course of events.

MONIQUE. How horrible! How can you say such awful things?

RUDY. (*soberly*) Because I need that money desperately! That man out there could have me beaten, tortured, maimed for life! If I don't pay what I owe, I'd be better off putting a bullet through my head!

MONIQUE. I prefer you in black comedy to melodrama!

RUDY. (*vexed*) I thought marriage would straighten me out. I see now, it's impossible. I'm a doomed man! (*He pours a large whiskey.*) I'm good for nothing but the furneral pyre! (*He drinks. Voices are heard offstage.*) Ah, here comes my nemesis now!

(*LOUISE shows Monsieur CORBEAU into the room. He's a rather distinguished looking man. His manner is easygoing but his eyes are made of steel.*)

RUDY. (*continued*) Come in, Monsieur Corbeau, come in!
CORBEAU. I hope I'm not disturbing you?
RUDY. Not at all! I'd like you to meet my wife, Monique. (*to her*) Monsieur Corbeau. He's a 'dear' friend. I owe him a great deal. (*The men laugh.*)
CORBEAU. (*pleasantly*) Your husband often talks about you, madame, but until now I've only had the pleasure of . . .
MONIQUE. (*interrupting*) What? Seeing my checks? Then you already know what's most interesting about me. (*an embarrassed pause*) For I suppose you, too, have investigated the size of my fortune?
CORBEAU. (*embarrassed*) No! It wasn't necessary! . . . There are rumors . . . the tom-toms of the credit jungle.
MONIQUE. Well, the tom-toms beat out the truth. But I have another message for the credit jungle. I no longer intend to cover my husband's debts!
CORBEAU. (*livid*) Rudy, you told me . . . ! That's a lot of money and I intend to get paid!
RUDY. My wife is joking! You'll be paid.
MONIQUE. Will he?
RUDY. Yes, he will. Where's your checkbook?
MONIQUE. Monsieur Corbeau, I have hidden my checkbook! (*to RUDY*) Well, aren't you going to hit me? As usual? I wish you would . . . in front of these two witnesses. It will make interesting testimony for the divorce!
CORBEAU. Madame, I'm sorry to disappoint you, but a man who is waiting for a check, can't afford to see or hear anything.

MONIQUE. (*icily*) Monsieur Corbeau, you are a gentleman!

CORBEAU. No, but I *am* in a hurry. And I need this money.

RUDY. And you'll get it! In two seconds! (*He glares at MONIQUE. Horrified, CORBEAU and LOUISE are glued to the spot. Suddenly, as RUDY takes a step towards MONIQUE, threatening her, LOUISE rushes forth, crying out:*)

LOUISE. Behind the picture! The checkbook is behind the picture!

RUDY. Well, why didn't you say so before! (*He feels behind the picture and finds the checkbook.*) Open, sesame! (*He opens the checkbook, puts it on the desk and picks up a pen. Then, he forces his wife to sit at the desk and puts the pen in her hand.*) And now, Ladies and Gentlemen, may I have complete silence while my wife, Monique Popesco, executes the difficult feat of parting with her money! How much is it, my dear Monsieur Corbeau? (*Delighted, CORBEAU goes to him.*)

CORBEAU. What you lost last night or everything you owe me?

RUDY. Everything, my friend, everything! What's another zero or two to a wealthy lady!

CORBEAU. (*consulting his notebook*) Let's see . . . altogether: one hundred and thirteen thousand francs.

RUDY. Did you hear that, my darling? One hundred and thirteen thousand. That's three zeros. (*Defeated, MONIQUE starts to write the check. RUDY, delighted, raises his glass and finishes off his whiskey. But suddenly, MONIQUE stops writing and, after an explosive silence, throws the pen away. RUDY is furious. He bangs his hand down on the desk, smashing the glass and cutting his hand. The blood spurts.*)

LOUISE. Oh! Monsieur has cut his hand! (*She gives him a napkin from the tray, which he wraps around his hand.*)

RUDY. (*to MONIQUE*) Perfect. That's perfect. We'll settle this between ourselves . . . later! (*He looks at her coldly, then decides to change his plan.*) My dear Corbeau, I must apologize for my wife's recalcitrance. But since she's adamant, I won't press her. Instead, would you accept a note from me, payable in forty-eight hours?

CORBEAU. Forty-eight hours?

RUDY. Yes, I still own some shares in my family's business in Marseilles. It's a very solid company.

CORBEAU. So I've been told.

RUDY. Well, just give me time to fly down there and sell the shares.

CORBEAU. I agree. I'm not a monster. But let's make sure we understand each other. Forty-eight hours. Not one second more!

RUDY. I'll make out the note to that effect. Come upstairs to my study, it will be quieter there. And while I'm about it, I'll pack my bag. (*to MONIQUE*) Will you miss me, my love? (*He looks at MONIQUE with hatred before going upstairs with CORBEAU. They exit. The study door is heard closing behind them. MONIQUE collapses at the desk, sobbing. LOUISE crosses to her.*)

LOUISE. Forgive me, madame, for telling him where you had hidden the checkbook! I came across it when I was dusting and I couldn't bear it if he hit you again!

MONIQUE. He controlled himself because of Corbeau. But later . . . when his friend leaves . . .

LOUISE. My God! I'm glad he cut his hand! It serves him right!

MONIQUE. (*suddenly remembering something*) Louise . . .
LOUISE. (*misunderstanding*) Well, I *am* glad!
MONIQUE. . . . You didn't answer my question.
LOUISE. Your question?
MONIQUE. The question I asked you before Rudy arrived.
LOUISE. (*turning red*) Oh! I . . . I must take the breakfast tray into the kitchen. (*She goes for the breakfast tray. MONIQUE grabs her arm, making LOUISE turn to face her.*)
MONIQUE. Stay here! . . . I asked you why my husband would be upset if you went away with Michel when he gets out of prison. You didn't answer me! My husband has a hold over you, is that it? Over you and your friend?
LOUISE. That's right.
MONIQUE. Who is this man? Why was he sent to prison? (*LOUISE doesn't answer. MONIQUE makes her sit beside her.*) Don't you trust me?
LOUISE. (*taking the plunge*) . . . Michel is in prison because of Rudy. He's paying for a crime Rudy committed. A jewel robbery.
MONIQUE. A jewel robbery?
LOUISE. Yes! Michel was arrested instead of Rudy.
MONIQUE. And Michel didn't say anything?
LOUISE. No.
MONIQUE. Why?
LOUISE. He was afraid. Naive, too. Michel sacrificed himself for Rudy.
MONIQUE. Sacrificed himself? You don't sacrifice yourself like that without a reason!
LOUISE. Well . . . Michel . . . he . . . he's Rudy's brother!
MONIQUE. But Rudy has no brother!

LOUISE. . . . Yes, he has! Michel!

MONIQUE. Rudy never mentioned a brother to me!

LOUISE. I know. And he warned me never to tell you.

MONIQUE. (*as though turned to stone, repeating it*) Rudy has a brother!

LOUISE. He's a year younger. Poor Michel! He always looked up to Rudy . . . admired him so much! That was his undoing. Rudy made him do everything he wanted!

MONIQUE. Wait! I can't make sense of it . . . Rudy has a brother! But, wait now, little things are coming back to me. One day in Venice, a woman asked Rudy how his brother was. Rudy told me she was crazy! And once he received a letter and the first name wasn't his. It seems to me . . . yes, it was indeed . . . Michel. And then there was a strange phone call for a . . . Michel. Yes, it makes sense. Rudy has a brother!

LOUISE. Yes, a brother he allowed to go to prison! And Michel and I love each other!

MONIQUE. Where did you meet him?

LOUISE. Here, in this house. He was one of Rudy's victims, like you are now. That's why Rudy mustn't know Michel is getting out of prison tomorrow. He'll get Michel under his thumb again and cause us all kinds of trouble!

MONIQUE. (*after a long pause; decisively*) Louise, we're going to muster our forces! I am going to fight. I don't know how yet, but I can promise you one thing: I'll help you leave tonight . . . unseen . . . and tomorrow you'll be in Fresnes to meet Michel. And I'm going to give you a check so you can take off at once to anywhere in the world you want to go . . . and good luck to you both!

LOUISE. (*touched but uneasy*) Madame! Oh, madame! But I can't leave you! Monsieur Rudy is capable of doing anything to get his hands on your money!

MONIQUE. Oh, the money is not important . . . Come now, calm down, Louise! And from now on, we mustn't appear to be too friendly. Rudy musn't suspect we're plotting against him.

LOUISE. Oh, no! . . . Oh, madame, when I tell Michel of your kindness . . . your generosity . . . it will give him new faith. Imagine going to prison because of your brother! It's disgusting!

MONIQUE. Sh! But tell me . . . why do you say . . . 'because of his brother?'

LOUISE. After holding up the jewelry store, Rudy, to save himself, stole Michel's alibi. Michel was playing cards at the time in the home of a friend. When the police picked him up, Michel, who is always so nervous, looked like he was guilty . . .

MONIQUE. But why didn't Michel defend himself in court? You did say he was arrested instead of Rudy.

LOUISE. Yes, he was arrested instead of Rudy because the witnesses believed and swore it was Michel they saw running out of the jewelry store.

MONIQUE. But how could the witnesses make that mistake? I don't understand.

LOUISE. Oh! I forgot to tell you the most important thing.

MONIQUE. The most important thing?

LOUISE. Yes. Rudy and Michel . . . resemble each other.

MONIQUE. Resemble each other?

LOUISE. Like two drops of water!

MONIQUE. What?

LOUISE. Yes! Though there's a year's difference between them, you have to really know them to tell them apart.

MONIQUE. They look alike?

Louise. A year's difference, but you'd think they're twins!
Monique. Ah!! Rudy has a double?
Louise. That's it. Rudy and Michel . . . they're doubles!

(*MONIQUE is startled by this revelation. A glint comes into her eyes. It must be made very clear to the audience that an idea is forming in her mind and she is about to get it together.*)

Monique. Rudy has a brother . . . and they look alike. Well, well, well!
Louise. But please, you won't say a word!
Monique. Oh, no! Not a word to Rudy! This is too marvelous! Too extraordinary! . . . Louise, will you do one thing for me?
Louise. Anything, madame! What is it?

(*A door slams. RUDY and CORBEAU are heard offstage. MONIQUE and LOUISE are startled and separate quickly. LOUISE exits into the kitchen with the breakfast tray. MONIQUE sits and leafs through a magazine. RUDY and CORBEAU appear. RUDY has a large but neat dressing on his hand. In the other, he carries a suitcase. CORBEAU is putting several papers into his wallet.*)

Corbeau. Well, all's well that ends well! Good contracts make good friends! In forty-eight hours, we'll never have to mention this again!
Rudy. (*to MONIQUE*) Your husband has been cut to bits, my darling! (*holding up his bandaged hand*) Not only physically . . . (*looking at CORBEAU*) but financially! (*He laughs.*)

CORBEAU. Can you call me a taxi?

RUDY. That won't be necessary! I'll drop you off in Paris on my way to the airport. I want to catch the eleven o'clock flight to Marseilles.

CORBEAU. Perfect! Thank you. (*Preening like a peacock, he goes to MONIQUE.*) I'm delighted to have met you at last, madame, but desolated at having disturbed you at this unseemly hour . . . and for being the cause of an unpleasant incident. (*Against all expectations, MONIQUE smiles at him graciously.*)

MONIQUE. There's no need to apologize, Monsieur Corbeau. It's a pity my husband has a temper and had too much to drink. I would have given him the money, you know. Such a modest sum. But there are nicer ways of asking for it, aren't there?

CORBEAU. I suppose there are.

RUDY. But, you see, my darling, it's time I started paying my own debts. I'll fly to Marseilles, sell my shares, and come right back to you . . .

MONIQUE. (*without faltering*) I'll be waiting! You will phone me, won't you?

RUDY. Every hour! I'll be so bored without you! . . . Oh, darling, now that we've made up . . . (*He kisses her on the neck.*) I must confess one little thing: I owe a hundred and ten thousand francs to a Brazilian! . . . He talked me into a deal, which, unfortunately, backfired. He'll be coming here tomorrow for his money . . . No! Don't get excited! I'm not asking you for the money! . . . Oh, you are touchy about your Swiss francs! (*indicating CORBEAU*) No, I've come to an arrangement with our friend here. We've added the hundred and ten thousand to the note I signed. The only reason I brought it up, my darling, is because Monsieur Corbeau will bring the money to the house tonight or tomorrow so you can give it to the Brazilian. Is that all right?

MONIQUE. Quite all right.

RUDY. Thank you.

CORBEAU. (*to MONIQUE*) When may I bring the money, madame, without disturbing you?

MONIQUE. Whenever you wish, monsieur. I won't be leaving the house.

CORBEAU. Shall we say tomorrow?

MONIQUE. Tomorrow will be fine. Anytime. (*She sits in a corner, turning her back to them, and leafs through her magazine.*)

RUDY. (*indicating the dressing on his hand*) And for the same amount of interest, Monsieur Corbeau has doctored my hand.

CORBEAU. It's an ugly cut. Make certain you change the bandage to avoid infection.

RUDY. I will, doctor!

CORBEAU. And be sure to call me from Marseilles as soon as you've sold the shares. I want to notify my bank.

RUDY. Of course!

CORBEAU. You won't have difficulty selling them?

RUDY. None! These are family shares!

CORBEAU. Well . . . that's exactly what I mean. Legally, you can't sell them without first getting your brother's consent.

(*At the mention of the word "brother," RUDY puts his hand over CORBEAU's mouth, startling him. Then, RUDY puts his finger to his own lips, a sign for CORBEAU to keep quiet because of his wife! However, the word "brother" strikes MONIQUE like a dagger in the back! Her eyes flash but she doesn't move.*)

Rudy. Consent? Consent? But I don't need my father's consent . . . (*calling out*) Louise! (*to CORBEAU*) My *father's* been dead six years!

Corbeau. (*baffled*) Oh? Yes. Well, so much the better . . . ! (*LOUISE enters.*)

Rudy. Take good care of madame while I'm gone, Louise.

Louise. Yes, monsieur. You can depend on me. (*LOUISE goes back up to the kitchen door but doesn't leave. RUDY crosses to MONIQUE.*)

Rudy. You haven't been very nice, Monique.

Monique. . . . And you haven't been very diplomatic! We're even.

Rudy. As soon as I get back, my darling, we'll plan a second honeymoon! I promise!

Monique. (*smiling*) You'll never change! . . . Oh! If I know you, you haven't a sou in your pocket. How do you expect to pay for your plane ticket and the hotel?

Rudy. By borrowing from Monsieur Corbeau.

Corbeau. (*shocked*) Again?!

Monique. (*smiling*) You're incorrigible!

Rudy. No. Insolvent. (*Meanwhile, MONIQUE has written him a check, which she shows him. When RUDY see the amount, he is amazed.*) I can't believe it! . . . This is very generous of you!

Monique. That's so you shouldn't be too bored without me. You can do a bit of gambling . . .

Rudy. Oh, I adore you! (*He takes MONIQUE in his arms and kisses her . . . a very sensual kiss. MONIQUE cannot resist; her body melts; then, she puts her hand behind RUDY's neck so she can prolong the kiss. When they break, RUDY asks cynically:*) And the check? (*She gives it to him.*) This *is* a surprise!

Monique. There's no end to a woman's surprises, my darling! (*All laugh. Then, RUDY picks up his suitcase.*)

RUDY. (*to CORBEAU*) Come along, my friend . . .
CORBEAU. Until tomorrow, madame! (*RUDY and CORBEAU exit by the terrace.*)
MONIQUE. (*changing the tone of her voice*) Quick, Louise! See what they're doing! But don't let them catch you looking! (*LOUISE goes up to the terrace and looks outside.*)
LOUISE. I've seen that man before. He's in the legal profession . . . Oh! They've stopped! Monsieur is angry! They're quarreling!
MONIQUE. (*smiling*) Of course! Corbeau made the mistake of mentioning the forbidden word . . . 'brother'
LOUISE. (*going to her*) Oh, my God!
MONIQUE. Don't worry, Louise. I didn't give the game away. Rudy doesn't suspect I know a thing! (*sound of the car driving off*)
LOUISE. Oh lalalala . . . I don't know how I'm going to last until tonight!
MONIQUE. You don't have to be afraid: my husband has left for Marseilles. He won't be back for two days.
LOUISE. Oh! That's true! I can leave safely and tomorrow at dawn I'll be waiting outside the prison gate!
MONIQUE. (*explicitly*) . . . With the money I promised you!
LOUISE. Oh, thank you again, madame!
MONIQUE. (*sweetly*) But I am going to ask you to do one thing for me . . .
LOUISE. Anything you want!
MONIQUE. After Michel gets out of prison tomorrow, bring him here.
LOUISE. Here! But that would be too dangerous!
MONIQUE. No, it wouldn't. I told you Rudy will be in Marseilles for two days. There's no risk!
LOUISE. But . . . why do you want to see Michel?
MONIQUE. (*with a false casualness*) I want to see him

... just to see him! I want to shake his hand ... wish him luck. (*rather diabolically*) Besides it will do me good ... to see you both happy.

LOUISE. But there'll hardly be time to ...

MONIQUE. (*interrupting*) What? Say 'hello and God be with you?' Fifteen minutes! That's all it will take!

LOUISE. (*giving in*) Very well! ... That is, I'll ask him if he wants to come.

MONIQUE. (*realistically*) I'll give you one hundred and fifty thousand francs!

LOUISE. (*stunned*) One hundred and fifty thousand francs?

MONIQUE. Yes ...

LOUISE. One hundred and fifty thousand for Michel and me?

MONIQUE. Yes!

LOUISE. One hundred and fifty thousand! Oh, I certainly made a wise move, telling you about Michel!

MONIQUE. (*slyly*) Very wise, indeed!

LOUISE. But ... what will happen to you when monsieur learns that I have gone?

MONIQUE. Nothing! When Rudy returns, he's going to find the sweetest, most submissive wife in the world waiting for him!

LOUISE. Oh? You're not bitter? You don't hate him?

MONIQUE. My dear Louise, the Bible tells us to turn the other cheek. And do you know why?

LOUISE. No.

MONIQUE. Because when the villain approaches to slap your other cheek, you are prepared.

LOUISE. Prepared?

MONIQUE. Prepared to play him a dirty trick!

BLACKOUT

Scene 2

The same, the following morning. The curtains are drawn, the room in darkness.

MONIQUE, in another expensive but simply-stated dress, comes down the stairs. She opens the curtains. Sunshine floods the room. MONIQUE stands at the window for a moment, simmering with impatience. She goes out on the terrace to see if anyone is coming . . . No one! Suddenly, the telephone rings.

MONIQUE. (*into the phone*) Hello? . . . Yes, that's right! . . . Marseilles? Yes, I'll hang on! . . . Yes, I'm still holding . . . (*then:*) Oh, Rudy, you called! Yes, I'm all right . . . Yes, yes, I assure you I'm all right! And you? Were you successful? I mean, in selling your shares? . . . Wonderful! . . . Oh, no, I read a bit, watched television. And you? . . . (*facetiously*) Four A.M.? You got to bed as early as that? You're improving! (*suddenly*) Louise? No, she isn't here . . . She's . . . gone . . . to the village . . . to do some shopping! Why do you want to speak to her? . . . Your diamond cuff links? She didn't say anything to me! Are you sure you didn't lose them in Marseilles last night . . . gambling? (*The sound of a car parking in the driveway is heard. Instinctively, MONIQUE puts her hand over the mouthpiece until the noise stops.*) . . . It's nothing to worry about! When you get back, I'll buy you another pair! (*LOUISE, wearing a raincoat, appears on the terrace. She is filled with apprehension.*) . . . Yes. So do I. I adore you! . . . Would I be waiting here like an unhappy Penelope if I didn't? . . . Yes. Until tomorrow. (*She hangs up and goes to LOUISE.*) Well? Well?

LOUISE. . . . Well . . .

MONIQUE. Did he get out of prison?

LOUISE. Yes! Michel is out of prison!
MONIQUE. Why isn't he with you?
LOUISE. He . . . he . . .
MONIQUE. (*impatiently*) You promised to bring him here!
LOUISE. . . . He's afraid.
MONIQUE. Afraid of what?
LOUISE. . . . that Rudy might be in the house . . . hiding.
MONIQUE. He's not. You heard. He just telephoned me from Marseilles! Oh, please, Louise, I must see him. Where is Michel?
LOUISE. Outside . . . in the taxi.
MONIQUE. (*furiously*) Oh, you gave me a fright! Go get him, Louise! Bring him in! (*LOUISE goes to the terrace.*)
LOUISE. (*calling*) Michel! . . . Michel, it's all right! You can come in! (*to MONIQUE*) He's trying to decide, madame! (*sound of the taxi leaving*) That's it! He's coming! . . . Michel! Hurry!

(*MICHEL enters. The first thing that strikes you, of course, is his resemblance to RUDY. But it is a purely physical resemblance for MICHEL is timid and naive . . . an appealing, beaten dog. His hair is neatly parted. Near-sighted, he wears glasses. His grey trousers are wrinkled, his sweater and cheap topcoat well-worn. He stands on the threshold, carrying his suitcase, looking about the room, and then, at MONIQUE.*)

LOUISE. (*making the introduction*) Michel . . . This is Rudy's wife. (*to MONIQUE*) Michel.
MONIQUE. (*holding out her hand to him*) I'm

delighted to meet you. My name is Monique. Has Louise told you everything?

MICHEL. Yes. Everything. Just now . . . Nobody told me Rudy was married. He forbid it! This is quite a surprise!

MONIQUE. You see, my dear Michel, while you were in prison, Rudy found himself another victim. But now that I know he has a brother. I decided I'd no longer let myself be . . . Oh. Won't you sit down? (*MICHEL, ill-at-ease, sits.*) Would you like a cup of coffee? Yes! Some good coffee. Louise, please . . . A cigarette? (*He refuses. LOUISE, very happy, exits into the kitchen with MICHEL's suitcase and topcoat. Alone with MICHEL, MONIQUE is overly sweet and sympathetic . . . the better to manipulate him.*) Louise told me how Rudy got you sent to prison, when it was he who committed the crime. What a shameful thing to do!

MICHEL. Yes, Rudy stole my alibi . . . and bribed my friend to lie for him. Can you imagine anyone doing that to his own brother? Until then, I had always admired Rudy . . . looked up to him.

MONIQUE. And now you hate him?

MICHEL. Oh, no. I could never go so far as to hate Rudy. It's not possible. You see, though there's only a year's difference between us, Rudy raised me!

MONIQUE. Raised you?

MICHEL. Yes. My father was in the army, stationed in the colonies. My mother was seldom home. I'd rather not talk about it. Rudy looked after me, taught me everything I know. I became his shadow! A friend explained it's a classic case. And there's no chance of a cure. I'll always be Rudy's victim because he's more intelligent than me, surer of himself, and the girls always ran after Rudy, while I . . .

MONIQUE. But Louise tells me she loves you, Michel!

MICHEL. (*brightening*) Yes, what luck! And I have proof that she loves me: every week I was in prison, she sent me a food package! When she first came to work here, I was afraid to speak to her. Then I found out she had the same problem: an older sister she admired, abandoned her to follow a guitar player to America. Only then did I dare speak to her . . . Louise and I are made for each other. We're two simple people, madame . . .

MONIQUE. Monique.

MICHEL. Yes. Two simple, honest people, who want to stay that way! . . . But it isn't easy to remain honest!

MONIQUE. (*touched*) Dear Michel. It's true you look like Rudy but how different you are!

MICHEL. That's what everyone says.

MONIQUE. He succeeded in sending you to prison . . . and he succeeded in marrying me.

MICHEL. A fine brother and a fine husband!

MONIQUE. Now he hopes to ruin me!

MICHEL. (*perplexed*) Ruin? Oh. Because you're rich?

MONIQUE. Yes. Very. Rudy wants to get control . . . or . . . why not? inherit my fortune. His aim is to destroy me. That's clear now. He won't stop at anything.

MICHEL. (*terrified*) You think so?

MONIQUE. He's capable of it, isn't he?

MICHEL. Yes, Rudy's capable of it.

MONIQUE. (*explicitly*) I had no defense against him. I was so infatuated, Rudy could do anything he wanted with me. That is, until yesterday, when your letter arrived . . . and I discovered he had a brother . . . a brother who looks like him . . . yes, really *does* look like him! It gave me an idea.

MICHEL. An idea?

MONIQUE. (*sweetly*) Yes. I suddenly realized that perhaps, thanks to you, I can . . . (*At this moment, LOUISE enters with a cup of coffee. MICHEL, delighted with the interruption, starts to drink. Prudently:*) While you drink your coffee, I'll explain my plan.

LOUISE. What plan?

MICHEL. (*looking up from his coffee*) Huh?

MONIQUE. . . . I mean, what I hope to do . . . (*to both MICHEL and LOUISE*) with your help.

LOUISE. Help?

MICHEL. Do what?

LOUISE. (*uneasily*) Oh, madame! Madame! What are you thinking of now? I kept my part of the bargain! You wanted to see Michel and you've seen him. Good. Now give us the money you promised so we can get away. Oh, madame! Please!

MONIQUE. (*incisively*) Help me! I'm Rudy's prisoner! I must be free of him . . . and I've found a solution . . . a simple one . . . I want a divorce.

MICHEL. Who's stopping you?

MONIQUE. Rudy! He'd rather kill me!

LOUISE. But what can we do?

MONIQUE. Everything. Michel can!

MICHEL. Me?

MONIQUE. Yes, Michel! Listen to me: Rudy took advantage of the fact you resemble him. Well, I'm going to use this resemblance to get the better of Rudy! Turn about is fair play. Listen carefully, Michel: for a few hours, you are going to be Rudy.

MICHEL. Be Rudy? What do you mean?

MONIQUE. (*ardently*) We'll see an attorney, a notary or whatever it is you call that official, and you'll declare that you . . . 'Rudy' . . . will accept a divorce. We'll sign the necessary papers . . . and I'll be free! We'll both be free! You and Louise can go anywhere in the world you want and I'll return to Switzerland! What do you say? (*a long pause*)

MICHEL. (*suddenly distraught*) No, no, no, no, no, it's too dangerous! I'd never be able to do it! No, no, I'm too clumsy! Any idiot could tell I'm not Rudy!

MONIQUE. You'll comb your hair like Rudy, wear his clothes, learn to imitate his signature . . .

MICHEL. No, no! Louise, say something!

LOUISE. (*suddenly shouting at him*) Sit down, Michel! You're making me dizzy! (*Intimidated, he sits.*) Let me think. We must consider the pros and cons. And a big argument against the idea is that Michel is not a good actor!

MONIQUE. He won't have to make a speech! All he has to do is be present. 'Rudy' will be in favor of the divorce so he won't have to say anything. He'll simply have to sign the papers, nothing more.

LOUISE. (*not wholly convinced*) Well. (*brightening*) But let's look at the arguments for the idea. How much?

MONIQUE. (*who doesn't understand*) How much what?

LOUISE. How much more are you offering us?

MONIQUE. (*a bit shocked*) Oh? Well, at least that's a step in the right direction. How much do you want?

LOUISE. How much do you think it's worth, madame?

MONIQUE. I don't know. Name a figure.

LOUISE. (*taking her courage in both hands*) . . . Three hundred and fifty thousand! Plus the hundred and fifty thousand you already promised. That's a total of half a million!

MICHEL. . . . Oh no, that's too much!

LOUISE. Be quiet! (*repeating to MONIQUE*) Half a million!

MONIQUE. (*breathing out*) Oooooooh! I underestimated you, Louise. You know how to profit from a situation, don't you?

LOUISE. Me? You're the one who's profiting from a situation, madame. I mean, from the resemblance of the two brothers. And who brought Michel to you? I did! If you hadn't pleaded with me, we'd already be on a plane for Madrid.

MICHEL. Madrid? Why Madrid?

LOUISE. Be quiet! (*to MONIQUE*) Well? Half a million? Is it a deal? It means nothing to you, madame. You're always talking about your Swiss fortune. Put it to work . . .

MONIQUE. Very well. Besides, I didn't intend to haggle.

LOUISE. Good.

MICHEL. But I . . .

LOUISE. Be quiet! (*She looks triumphantly at MICHEL, before turning to MONIQUE.*) Now madame, how and when are you giving us the money?

MONIQUE. You fixed the price so fix the method of payment.

LOUISE. Twenty-five percent now. Another twenty-five percent when Michel starts to rehearse his role . . . twenty-five percent just before your official arrives and the final payment when he leaves. Is that all right?

MONIQUE. Perfect.

LOUISE. (*to MICHEL, delighted*) Did you hear that?

MICHEL. Yes, I heard, but you don't give me time to think! . . . No! I say no!

LOUISE. No to half a million? Don't you love me, Michel?

MICHEL. I'm just out of prison. If something goes wrong, I'll be sent back for ten years! No! No, thank you very much! (*LOUISE looks at MONIQUE, then suddenly turns on MICHEL.*)

LOUISE. Michel, you're a coward! Afraid of your own shadow!

MICHEL. What?

LOUISE. You'll never have another chance like this and you want to throw it away! Well, go back to your job in the cannery!

MICHEL. (*getting red in the face*) What's come over you?

LOUISE. I've had enough! Enough of being a maid, enough of poverty, enough of canneries, enough of *you*!

MICHEL. (*beside himself*) Be quiet! Be quiet!

LOUISE. No! I will not be quiet! You're nothing but a weakling, born to lose and lose and lose!

MICHEL. Don't talk to me like that! You're making me angry and if I lose my temper . . .

LOUISE. You don't frighten me!

MICHEL. Oh, no?! (*In a rage, MICHEL picks up and brandishes a chair, threatening LOUISE. LOUISE, suddenly becoming calm again, turns to MONIQUE and points to MICHEL.*)

LOUISE. There. You see?

MONIQUE. (*with sudden realization*) Y-e-s! That's it!

MICHEL. What?

MONIQUE. Rudy . . . I thought I was seeing Rudy! That's wonderful, Louise!

LOUISE. You see, Michel, it won't be difficult to do what we're asking. All you need is a little prodding!

MONIQUE. When he gets angry, his face contorts like Rudy's! It's striking! (*Bewildered, MICHEL looks at them, moans softly and sits, vanquished.*)

Louise. (*kisses MICHEL*) With just a little effort, my darling, you will make us half a million francs!

Monique. Let's stop talking of money. We're agreed on that and it's not important. What is important, Michel, is that you do your duty and free us all from Rudy! You must help me . . . please!

Michel. (*hesitates, then . . .*) All right. I'll do it.

Monique. Oh, thank you, Michel! Thank you!

Louise. That's marvelous!

Michel. But you'll have to coach me . . . or I'll make a mess of it!

Monique. You can count on us, Michel. We'll help in every way we can! (*MICHEL puts his head in his hands, ready to sob. MONIQUE and LOUISE look at him and realize it's not going to be as easy as they thought.*)

Louise. Finish your coffee . . .

Monique. Yes, and we'll get to work . . . (*She exits upstairs to the bedrooms.*)

Louise. Come on, Michel. Everything will be all right. Drink your coffee . . . Come on now. (*MICHEL drinks the coffee. MONIQUE returns with a handsome dressing gown.*)

Monique. Take off his glasses, Louise! (*LOUISE does so.*)

Michel. (*crying out*) No! I can't see! I'm near-sighted!

Louise. With half a million francs in sight, you can see far enough! (*MONIQUE displays the dressing gown and hands it to MICHEL.*)

Monique. Stand up, Michel, and put on Rudy's dressing gown . . . (*He does as he is told. MONIQUE, judging the effect, concludes:*) Extraordinary!

Louise. Wait! His hair! (*She combs it RUDY's way.*) There!

Monique. (*admiring the change*) Oh, yes! . . .

Michel, walk around . . . (*MICHEL tries to move with manly grace but is not very successful.*)

LOUISE. (*shouting at him*) No! Looser . . . free and easy!

MICHEL. But I don't feel free and easy! . . . No! I can't do it! It's hopeless! I'm giving up! (*They are about to start arguing with MICHEL again, when suddenly:*)

CORBEAU. (*off-stage*) Madame Popesco? May I come in? (*The trio panics. MICHEL tries to run away but LOUISE grabs him and forces him to sit behind the desk. CORBEAU enters from the terrace, carrying a briefcase. Crossing to MONIQUE:*) May I come in, madame?

MONIQUE. Oh, I didn't expect you . . . so soon!

CORBEAU. You said any time, madame. I left my car outside the gate and walked across the lawn . . . (*He sees MICHEL at the desk.*) . . . Rudy! What a surprise! I thought you were in Marseilles!

MICHEL. (*stammering*) Er . . . yes . . . (*He tries to hide his face with his hand.*)

MONIQUE. (*intervening*) Rudy came home earlier than expected . . . (*lowering her voice*) He's not well . . . he's been drinking! . . . Won't you sit down? (*She indicates a chair as far away from MICHEL as possible. Meanwhile, LOUISE pours a large cognac and hands it to MICHEL, who gulps it down to give himself courage. CORBEAU watches.*)

CORBEAU. (*low, to MONIQUE*) Stop a wild animal from drinking and he attacks! (*He opens his briefcase.*) I have brought the one hundred and ten thousand . . .

MONIQUE. Good! I'll give it to the Brazilian . . . (*She holds out her hand.*)

CORBEAU. . . . Well, since your husband is here . . . (*He takes out a bundle of bills.*)

MONIQUE. But I can . . .

CORBEAU. (*crossing to MICHEL*) It's not necessary. I can do it myself in a second! (*He sits facing MICHEL and puts the money on the desk. MICHEL looks scared.*) Here's the hundred and ten thousand . . .

MICHEL. (*coughing and clearing his throat*) uhuh-uhuh . . . oh? oh?

CORBEAU. Did everything go well in Marseilles? (*Behind CORBEAU's back, MONIQUE and LOUISE nod "yes."*)

MICHEL. . . . Yes!

CORBEAU. Splendid! Then I can consider the money as good as in my bank? (*Just as MONIQUE is about to nod "yes," CORBEAU looks at her, so MICHEL doesn't know what to answer.*)

MONIQUE. Yes, everything's in order. You can take my word for it. (*The bottle of cognac is on the desk. MICHEL re-fills his glass and tosses it down. CORBEAU watches him.*) My God, Rudy! Stop drinking or you'll pass out! . . . Do me a favor, go to bed and sleep for an hour or two!

CORBEAU. An excellent idea! . . . But before you go, my dear Rudy, sign the receipt for the hundred and ten thousand.

(*As CORBEAU returns to the sofa to look for the receipt in his briefcase, MONIQUE desperately pantomimes to LOUISE that MICHEL must hide his hand because there's no wound nor dressing on it! Quickly LOUISE whispers in MICHEL's ear but he doesn't understand. Finally, LOUISE grabs MICHEL's hand and thrusts it into his pocket.*)

MICHEL. (*to LOUISE, bewildered by these events*) What are you doing?

CORBEAU. What? I'm getting the receipt so you can

sign it. You know the procedure. You've signed enough of them! Here, on the dotted line! (*And he puts the receipt under his nose.*)

MICHEL. (*in a daze, not knowing what to do, then . . .*) I don't feel well, Louise!

MONIQUE. (*intervening quickly*) Oh, Rudy! . . . Louise, help me get monsieur upstairs. (*to MICHEL*) You'll feel better once you lie down. (*to LOUISE*) He must get some sleep . . . quickly and for as long as possible! (*MONIQUE and LOUISE help MICHEL to the foot of the staircase. CORBEAU, the unsigned receipt in hand, is not happy to see his man getting out of the room.*)

CORBEAU. My dear Rudy, but first you must . . .

MONIQUE. I'll be with you in a second, Monsieur Corbeau!

CORBEAU. You're very kind, madame, but . . .

LOUISE. (*to MICHEL*) Come on, monsieur, don't be difficult! Upstairs!

CORBEAU. . . . The signature!

MONIQUE. I'll sign the receipt, don't worry!

CORBEAU. . . . But since your husband is here . . . it's foolish! . . . (*to MICHEL*) My dear friend . . . (*But his "dear friend" can only make the vaguest acknowledgement as LOUISE has hurried MICHEL up the stairs. The bedroom door slams.*)

MONIQUE. (*going to CORBEAU*) Monsieur Corbeau, I'm terribly sorry Rudy made such a spectacle of himself. I don't know what to do. Every day he drinks more and more! (*CORBEAU impatiently looks at his receipt, then at his watch.*) Oh! I'm delaying you! I'll sign the receipt . . . and that makes me personally responsible for the hundred and ten thousand, doesn't it? (*with a little laugh*) Well, I have the money!

Corbeau. I know you do, madame, I know you do. (*MONIQUE signs the receipt and hands it to CORBEAU.*)

Monique. There.

Corbeau. (*pocketing the receipt*) Thank you. To tell the truth, the only reason I started extending credit to your husband again was because he married you.

Monique. How charming!

Corbeau. What can you expect, madame? In my practise, prudence is the rule.

Monique. (*acting surprised*) . . . Your practise?

Corbeau. (*pompously*) Yes. Hasn't your husband told you about 'Monsieur Corbeau, Certified Legal Documents?' (*putting on airs*) My office is on the Champs-Elysees in Paris.

Monique. You're a lawyer?

Corbeau. Not quite, madame. I draw up documents and certify the facts contained therein to be true. I'm more than a notary but something less than an attorney.

Monique. How marvelous! I *am* impressed!

Corbeau. You're very kind!

Monique. I never dreamed you could be an arm of the legal profession . . . since you frequent the gambling tables with my husband.

Corbeau. Because I'm sworn to uphold the ethics of my profession, doesn't mean I'm not human. I have my weaknesses, like all men, but thank God, I'm honest, which is why I try to keep my equilibrium . . . I mean, my financial equilibrium.

Monique. (*quickly perceptive*) You're not, by any chance, having money problems, are you?

Corbeau. (*a bit shamefaced*) . . . Oh! Temporarily! That's why I insist on being paid what Rudy owes me.

Monique. Well, since your equilibrium is a bit off

balance, I have something to propose.

CORBEAU. (*pricking up his ears*) Oh? What is it? (*They sit and look at each other with fixed smiles, each on the defensive.*) You were saying?

MONIQUE. I need an affidavit. I think that's what it's called. And it's what you do, isn't it?

CORBEAU. Quite right. I attest to sworn statements.

MONIQUE. My husband, as you know is a brute. He beats me, robs me, and you have seen it with your own eyes. Can you attest to this?

CORBEAU. Me? Swear to myself that what I saw was true? But my dear Madame Popesco, I came to this house as your husband's friend, not in a professional capacity. I'm sorry!

MONIQUE. I understand. That's why I thought of a simpler solution to my problem.

CORBEAU. A simple solution is always to be preferred!

MONIQUE. Rudy and I will get a divorce.

CORBEAU. A divorce?

MONIQUE. Yes. I'll take the blame. And you'll draw up the affidavit.

CORBEAU. (*ironically*) My dear lady, a divorce can only be obtained with the consent of both parties! Will Rudy sign? . . . I doubt it!

MONIQUE. Don't! Rudy agrees! And he'll tell you so himself! Believe me, he'll sign!

CORBEAU. (*convinced*) Well, well, well! Congratulations! . . . It must have cost you a bundle. (*He winks.*)

MONIQUE. Freedom knows no price. When can you return with the necessary papers? The quicker the better!

CORBEAU. (*delighted and servile*) How about early this afternoon?

MONIQUE. That would be perfect. It gives me time to prepare . . . (*looking towards the bedroom*) Rudy . . . I mean, get him into shape.

CORBEAU. I'll spare you a course in the Civil Code, madame, but as soon as I get your signatures, I'll take the papers to a friend who specializes in divorce. It will be smooth sailing! (*He rubs his hands together, then looks at is watch.*) I'll see you at two o'clock then . . . with the papers.

MONIQUE. And I'll see you with my checkbook! As usual! It's my breviary!

CORBEAU. You fill me with admiration, madame! Yesterday, I left you a desperate woman, a victim of your husband's cruelty and greed. I pitied you. And today, I find you a new woman! Firm, decisive . . .

MONIQUE. That's because, since yesterday, I discovered the vital element I was missing.

CORBEAU. What's that?

MONIQUE. Courage!

CORBEAU. My congratulations again, madame! (*He bows and kisses her hand.*) I'll see you promptly at two.

MONIQUE. We'll be waiting! (*CORBEAU exits. LOUISE and MICHEL enter quickly.*) Did you hear?

LOUISE. Everything! Our ears were glued to the door!

MONIQUE. Two signatures, that's all we need!

LOUISE. Wonderful!

MICHEL. (*clogged with fear*) Oh, my God! My God!

LOUISE. 'Oh, my God! My God!' Is that all you can say? Turning green with fright in front of Corbeau! If I hadn't rushed you up to the bedroom . . .

MONIQUE. (*diplomatically*) Louise, don't pick on him. Michel was taken by surprise! It was a terrible spot to be in. I think he extricated himself beautifully!

MICHEL. (*to LOUISE*) There! You see!

MONIQUE. It was perfectly natural for him to be upset! Besides, Monsieur Corbeau believed he was drunk.

MICHEL. But when he comes back with the divorce papers and I have to *be* Rudy, what then?

MONIQUE. Monsieur Corbeau accepted you without hesitation. You've passed the most difficult test! There's no danger.

MICHEL. No? Then why do I feel sick? (*He sits.*)

MONIQUE. I have a prescription to make you feel better.

MICHEL. A prescription? (*MONIQUE writes a check and tears it out of the book.*)

MONIQUE. The first check, as promised.

LOUISE. Thank you, madame. (*She takes the check and reads it.*) That's perfect! Pay to the bearer.

MONIQUE. Now we must get ready for when Monsieur Corbeau returns.

LOUISE. Excuse me, madame. The second check. The one we get when Michel starts rehearsing.

MONIQUE. (*ironicaly, looking at LOUISE*) Excuse me. (*She writes the check.*)

LOUISE. There's no need to apologize, madame. (*She looks at MICHEL triumphantly. Then to MONIQUE:*) Made payable, of course, 'to bearer.' (*MONIQUE detaches the check but, as LOUISE reaches out to take it, MONIQUE smiles.*)

MONIQUE. No! . . . This check is for Michel. He certainly earned it. (*She offers the check to MICHEL, who turns to stone under LOUISE's gaze.*)

MICHEL. Oh, no! No! I . . .

MONIQUE. I insist. It will give you courage!

MICHEL. Courage? . . . Yes. Thanks. (*Delighted, he takes the check.*)

LOUISE. (*annoyed*) Try not to lose it!

MICHEL. I won't. (*With a chuckle, he puts the check in his pocket.*)

MONIQUE. (*to ease the friction*) And you'll get the third check before Corbeau arrives . . . and the fourth after he leaves.

LOUISE. (*brightening*) Yes! As we agreed!

MICHEL. Oh, no! It's too much!

LOUISE. What do you mean too much? It's never too much!

MICHEL. . . . I mean: so much money scares me!

MONIQUE. Don't be afraid, Michel, and don't have scruples. By tricking Rudy into this divorce, you're saving my life!

LOUISE. I must say, you amazed me, madame, the way you led Monsieur Corbeau up the garden path.

MONIQUE. I amazed myself! But as the Chinese proverb says: 'Fear gives a snail wings!' But we must hurry. We have only three hours. Michel, go up to Rudy's bedroom and change into his clothes. From head to toe.

MICHEL. All right, all right. (*He puts on his glasses and reluctantly starts up the stairs. He stops and turns.*) . . . But how should I dress? What should I put on?

MONIQUE. Oh, Rudy would be dressed for a day in the country.

MICHEL. (*grumbling*) A day in the country. What would I know about a day in the country after eleven months in jail! (*He exits. The bedroom door slams.*)

LOUISE. Michel is a hard man to convince!

MONIQUE. But we did it! And I want to thank you, Louise, for your help. Without you, he'd never have agreed to impersonate Rudy!

LOUISE. (*realistically*) There's no need to thank me. What's good for madame is good for Louise.

MONIQUE. That's true! Now let's get ready for Monsieur Corbeau. First, we must . . . (*crying out*) Oh! See that Michel puts a bandage on his hand! Don't forget!

LOUISE. Oh, I nearly died of fright when Corbeau . . . ! Trust me, madame, I'll take care of it at once. (*She opens a drawer, takes out a pair of scissors and a roll of adhesive plaster, which she prepares to cut into strips. The telephone rings. MONIQUE picks up the receiver. LOUISE listens.*)

MONIQUE. Hello? . . . Yes, that's right . . . (*to LOUISE*) Long distance, Bouches-du-Rhone! It's Rudy! (*a pause; into phone*) Thank you, operator . . . Yes . . . Rudy! How lovely of you to call again so soon! . . . Oh, no, there's nothing new here. Your friend Corbeau brought the hundred and ten thousand . . . What? I can't hear you. There's a noise . . . What? . . . You're phoning from where? . . . The airport? (*pause; to LOUISE*) He's flying to Paris in fifteen minutes!

LOUISE. No! He can't! (*MONIQUE takes a deep breath.*)

MONIQUE. (*into phone*) Why are you coming back so soon? . . . Oh . . . I'll have Louise prepare lunch for one o'clock then . . . Of course, I'm pleased. Very pleased. I couldn't be happier . . . See you soon . . . So do I! (*She hangs up.*)

LOUISE. What did he say?

MONIQUE. He'll be here in two hours.

LOUISE. Why?

MONIQUE. I don't know why! He was in a hurry! . . . He said he'll explain when he gets here!

LOUISE. How awful!

MONIQUE. (*frightened*) Rudy will be here in two hours! (*They look at each other appalled by this unexpected turn of events.*)

LOUISE. We can't stay. Michel and I must leave at

once. And you must call Monsieur Corbeau and tell him not to come here.

MONIQUE. (*finding her strength*) No! Never! Our plan is too good! I can't give it up!

LOUISE. But what can you do? Monsieur Rudy is coming back! You know how shrewd he is. He'll sense something is wrong and smash everything in sight until he finds out what it is!

MONIQUE. No! Rudy won't smash anything! I'll greet him calmly . . . and then . . . and then . . .

LOUISE. And then, what? . . . Nothing!

MONIQUE. (*searching for an idea*) No! I must find some way to get Rudy out of the way!

LOUISE. How?

MONIQUE. How? How? How? . . . Yes! My sleeping pills! When Rudy arrives, he'll ask for his whiskey, as usual . . . and then . . . !

LOUISE. What?

MONIQUE. Very simple. Enough in his whiskey to put him to sleep quickly! Then we'll drag him into the kitchen and lock the door!

LOUISE. (*frightened*) Oh, simple . . . very simple!

MONIQUE. Yes! Then we proceed as planned! Actually, there'll be less danger.

LOUISE. What do you mean 'less danger?'

MONIQUE. That phone call was a blessing in disguise! Rudy could have returned without warning and surprised us right in the middle of our plot. Now we can put Rudy out of action before Corbeau arrives. All the cards are in our hands!

LOUISE. (*a bit reassured by MONIQUE's passionate conviction*) . . . Maybe you're right.

MONIQUE. I am right. Now prepare lunch, Louise, just like any other day.

LOUISE. Ah la la la la la!

MONIQUE. Am I to gather from that that your morale is still low?
LOUISE. Yes, madame.
MONIQUE. Well, it will rise again.
LOUISE. When?
MONIQUE. When you think of the checks!
LOUISE. (*brightening*) You're right, madame! (*She goes towards the kitchen. But, suddenly, she turns back and hits her forehead with the palm of her hand.*) Oh! What about Michel?
MONIQUE. What about him? Nothing has changed as far as he's concerned.
LOUISE. You're joking! If he learns Rudy is on his way, he'll lose his head and scoot off like a frightened rabbit! I know Michel! (*thinking it over*) . . . And yet it's too risky not to tell him! What shall we do? What?
MONIQUE. We must tell him the truth! But, at the same time, double his confidence! Nothing must go wrong now! Help me, Louise!
LOUISE. I'll do everything I can. (*The bedroom door slams.*)
MONIQUE. Here he comes!

(*MICHEL comes downstairs, dressed in RUDY's clothes, but they are a little large for him. And, of course, MICHEL doesn't know how to wear them. NOTE: Two sets of this suit must be used by the actor playing the dual role. With one set too large, MICHEL will appear to the audience as being thinner than RUDY.*)

MICHEL. I'm swimming around in these clothes . . . I'm not built like Rudy, am I?
LOUISE. Leave the jacket open. There! Sit down.

(*MICHEL sits.*) The important thing is: do you feel more like Rudy?

MICHEL. Oh, that's coming along! Look! (*Imitating RUDY, he crosses his legs . . . clumsily.*) Well?

MONIQUE. (*to give him confidence*) Very good, Michel! Bravo! . . . But you must take off your glasses! (*She takes them off for him.*) There! Perfect!

LOUISE. And put this in your mouth . . . (*She puts one of RUDY's cigarillos in his mouth.*)

MICHEL. I don't like to smoke. It makes me cough.

LOUISE. Don't worry! Just three puffs . . . a signature . . . and we're rich! (*She lights the cigarillo.*)

MONIQUE. My God! His signature! (*to MICHEL*) Can you imitate Rudy's signature? I mean, a reasonable facsimile?

MICHEL. Oh, yes, that's nothing! I shouldn't boast, but Rudy often had me endorse checks for him . . . Look! (*He takes a sheet of paper and, with a flourish, signs RUDY's name.*) How's that?

MONIQUE. Yes! . . . But your R is too large and the P too legible . . .

MICHEL. Oh? (*He writes RUDY's name again.*)

LOUISE. (*who is also looking over his shoulder*) No! The stroke under Popesco is too long!

MICHEL. Oh! (*He writes RUDY's name for a third time. MONIQUE and LOUISE are a bit more satisfied.*)

MONIQUE. Perfect, Or, almost!

LOUISE. Yes, you still have time to practise!

MICHEL. I will . . . (*looking at the signatures*) It's funny, though, how much my signature resembles Rudy's. I suppose that's because I always wanted to copy everything about him. (*The women consult each other with a look, then decide to proceed.*)

MONIQUE. (*cautiously*) There's been a little change, Michel . . . (*MICHEL looks up.*) Oh, not for you!

LOUISE. Oh, no! Not for you! For you, everything stays the same!

MICHEL. Oh, good! . . . What is it?

MONIQUE. Well . . . in about two hours . . . Rudy will be here. (*Choking on his cigar, MICHEL, terrified, jumps. LOUISE uses both hands to keep him in his chair.*)

LOUISE. Ohhhhh! Stop trembling! Rudy won't be a threat for long!

MONIQUE. I'm putting something in his drink and, when he falls asleep, we'll lock him in the kitchen!

LOUISE. You see, it's nothing! A detail!

MONIQUE. Everything stays the same for you!

MICHEL. (*moaning*) Oh, it's a mistake! I'll be sent back to prison!

MONIQUE. Nonsense! You'll be a free man after today! Really free!

MICHEL. In any case, I don't want to be around when you put the stuff in his drink.

LOUISE. I promise! I won't call you until after Rudy passes out!

MICHEL. I'll hide at the bottom of the garden, behind the mulberry bush, against the old well, under the ivy . . . It's my private nook!

LOUISE. That's right! And don't forget to take an old blanket to lie on. You could soil your clothes!

MICHEL. Go ahead, make fun of me!

MONIQUE. Come now! There's no time to lose! We must decide what we're going to say and do when Monsieur Corbeau arrives. (*She issues her directives.*) Michel, at the desk, looking very pleased with yourself . . . cigarillo in hand. (*She installs MICHEL behind the*

desk accordingly.) Louise, you'll be at the kitchen door
. . . carrying a tray!

LOUISE. Why?

MONIQUE. It's after lunch! You'll be serving coffee!

LOUISE. Yes, of course! Two o'clock!

MONIQUE. Here's your tray. (*She hands LOUISE a magazine to use.*) Let's see . . . Michel and I will be chatting . . . (*She mimes the scene.*) 'Blah blah blah blah blah. Yes, Rudy! Ah, here's our coffee. Thank you, Louise . . . (*Suddenly, she looks towards the terrace, and darts forth, calling out:*) Oh, come in, Monsieur Corbeau!'

LOUISE. (*terrified, drops the magazine*) Oh!

MICHEL. (*in a panic, rises, wanting to flee*) He's here already?!

MONIQUE. (*impatiently*) No! I was pretending! . . . This is only a rehearsal! (*She sees the magazine LOUISE has dropped.*) There goes our coffee! Well, let's carry on . . . (*LOUISE and MICHEL take their places.*) 'My dear Monsieur Corbeau! Two o'clock. So prompt! Do come in and sit down . . . Are the papers ready? Rudy can't wait to sign them. Can you, darling? . . . Lovely weather we're having, isn't it? . . . Rudy, my darling, the papers . . . Rudy, you do want to sign the divorce papers, don't you?' (*Unnerved by MICHEL's silence, she strikes the desk with her fist.*) Speak! Say something! Here I am, jabbering away, and you sit there like a mummy! (*She immediately regrets her outburst.*) I'm sorry . . . I'm nervous, too . . .

MICHEL. (*timidly*) What should I say? Tell me what you want me to say.

MONIQUE. (*quickly but clearly*) Listen! You must reassure Corbeau you know what you're doing. When he saw you earlier, you were rather 'sloshed!' That's a word Rudy uses. But now, after your nap, you're . . . 'fresh as a daisy.'

MICHEL. Good. I understand. 'Fresh as a daisy!'

MONIQUE. (*rushing on*) Then bring up the divorce, our quarrels, which are growing worse, getting to be ridiculous. Then ask where to sign, but before that . . .

MICHEL. (*overwhelmed*) Wait! Not so fast! Not all at once, please!

MONIQUE. All right. We'll try this. I'll be Corbeau! And you, Louise, can be me. (*She goes to the door and, with considerable ease, plays CORBEAU. She kisses LOUISE's hand.*) I hope I'm not disturbing you, dear Madame Popesco?

LOUISE. (*a bit bewildered*) No . . . dear . . . monsieur . . .

MONIQUE. Ah! Rudy! How are you? . . . How are you? (*unnerved*) How are you, Rudy!

MICHEL. Not bad . . . not too bad!

MONIQUE. No! 'I'm feeling better! Much better! Very much better!'

MICHEL. Yes . . . 'scuse me.

MONIQUE. (*correcting his pronunciation*) Excuse me . . .

MICHEL. Yes . . . Because this morning I was rather . . . rather . . . rather . . . (*He searches for the word.*)

LOUISE. (*whispering*) Sloshed!

MICHEL. Sloshed! I had one two many! But now . . . after my nap . . . I'm . . . I'm . . . (*He searches for the phrase, suddenly remembers it, and says proudly:*) 'Fresh as a daisy!' (*Pleased, he puffs on his cigar . . . and chokes. MONIQUE and LOUISE look at him, uneasily.*)

BLACKOUT

Scene 3

The same, one hour later. MICHEL is rehearsing, with MONIQUE and LOUISE looking on.

MICHEL. Ah, Corbeau! How are you? I must apologize for being rather 'sloshed' this morning, but now that I've had a nap, I'm 'fresh as a daisy!' . . . What? Yes, of course, I agree to the divorce! Quarreling with Monique each and every day is ridiculous . . . and depressing! Where do you want me to sign? . . . Fine . . . There! . . . It's your turn, my darling! . . . As a wise man one said: 'The best thing about marriage is the divorce!'

(*A metamorphosis has taken place. The resemblance to RUDY is truly remarkable. Relaxed, in complete control, MICHEL puffs on his cigarillo but, alas, he coughs again. However, he puts out the cigarillo in an astray on the mantelpiece, and sits triumphantly.*)

MONIQUE. (*delighted*) Michel, that was marvelous!
LOUISE. (*approving*) You're wonderful! I could have sworn you were Rudy!
MONIQUE. Monsieur Corbeau will be royally deceived! Michel, I congratulate you!
MICHEL. (*swaggering*) Bah! It was nothing! Absolutely nothing! (*But suddenly he is terrified and becomes his poor self again.*) What time is it?
LOUISE. (*uneasily*) A quarter to one!
MONIQUE. Well, that's all the time we've got. Rudy's plane must have landed at Orly airport twenty minutes ago! . . . I must get the sleeping pills! (*She exits upstairs into the bedroom, leaving the door open.*)

LOUISE. Now it's up to you, madame . . .
MONIQUE. (*off-stage*) Yes, it's up to me . . .
MICHEL. (*trembling, as he puts on his glasses*) Can I go now and hide at the bottom of the garden?
LOUISE. Yes . . .
MICHEL. You'll call me when you need me, I suppose?
LOUISE. Yes . . .
MICHEL. Not before!
LOUISE. No!
MICHEL. (*calling up to MONIQUE*) Good luck, madame!
MONIQUE. (*off-stage*) To you, too, Michel!
MICHEL. Thanks! . . . Take care, Loulou!
LOUISE. I promise! (*MICHEL starts to leave.*) Wait! . . . Wouldn't you rather hide in the cellar?
MICHEL. (*shocked by the idea*) Lock myself in a cellar the first day I'm out of prison? No, thanks! (*He leaps over the terrace balustrade and disappears into the garden. MONIQUE re-appears on the staircase.*)
MONIQUE. I have the sleeping pills . . . (*She shows the bottle to LOUISE.*) They're very strong! . . . One pill and five minutes later you're dead to the world!
LOUISE. If I were you, madame, I'd give him the whole bottle to play safe.
MONIQUE. Listen! Rudy always takes his whiskey 'on the rocks' . . . (*She checks the bar.*) Louise, ice cubes! Quickly! (*LOUISE exits into the kitchen. MONIQUE arranges the bar: whiskey, glasses, etc. LOUISE returns with a bucket of ice.*) Thank you. One last problem. Will the pill dissolve rapidly and without leaving a trace? That's the danger. Well, let's find out. (*describing her actions*) I'll put the ice in the glass . . . pour the whiskey over it . . . and slip in the pill. There! You didn't see anything, did you?

LOUISE. I'm no judge, madame. I know what you're doing! (*They look more closely at the glass.*)
MONIQUE. It looks all right to me!
LOUISE. Yes! It dissolved without making a bubble! Amazing! (*They are delighted.*)
MONIQUE. Oh! The most important thing! How do we get rid of . . .

(*At this moment, a car comes screeching to a halt in the driveway. The horn gaily sounds "shave and a haircut." The car door slams. From a distance, RUDY shouts:* 'Darling! I'm home!')

MONIQUE. (*continued*) He's here! Already!

(*They are distraught. LOUISE retreats to the kitchen, taking the drugged whiskey glass with her. Before leaving, she crosses her fingers to ward off evil. MONIQUE sits. RUDY, in high spirits and with the perennial cigarillo in his mouth, enters. There's a new dressing on his hand. He puts down his suitcase and his topcoat.*)

RUDY. Darling, what are you doing over there?
MONIQUE. (*smiling, crosses to him*) Welcome home!
RUDY. It's lovely to see you, my darling! (*He kisses her.*) Aaaah! It was a marvelous trip. Even the plane was ten minutes early!
MONIQUE. So much the better!
RUDY. But what a time I had selling my shares! But it's done! And now we can start over again on a new footing! Ah! How good it is to be back home! (*He sits on the sofa, stretching out comfortably.*)
MONIQUE. Back in your own home . . . with a wife,

who adores you . . . not to mention your own whiskey! Your cup runneth over! (*She goes to the bar to pour his whiskey.*) . . . But why did you come back from Marseilles so soon?

RUDY. To tell the truth, my love . . . last night I ran into a little problem at the gaming tables with a Corsican bandit. He suggested that I get out of Marseilles immediately. He was so 'charming' I didn't have the heart to refuse him. Besides, the weather was dismal and the hotel foul. So I rushed home to be with my guardian angel! (*During this, MONIQUE has drugged his drink. She offers it to him.*)

MONIQUE. Here's your whiskey . . . 'on the rocks,' the way you like it!

RUDY. You're a love! But . . . no, thank you!

MONIQUE. (*nailed to the spot*) Really? . . . How sensible! Why?

RUDY. The doctor, who changed the dressing in Marseilles, gave me antibiotics. He said to stay away from alcohol.

MONIQUE. Oh? Your hand still bothers you?

RUDY. (*indicating his bandaged hand*) There's a slight infection. It stings. So, no more whiskey!

MONIQUE. What a pity . . . it's poured.

RUDY. Then, you drink it! Drink to my health!

MONIQUE. Oh, no! . . . You know me and whiskey! (*She shudders and makes a face.*) Tonight you can start following doctor's orders. Here, drink it, and then we'll have lunch.

RUDY. Temptress! Well, tough luck, old hand! (*He takes the glass. MONIQUE cannot suppress a sigh of relief.*) Aren't you taking a drop with me?

MONIQUE. Well, only a drop . . . (*She goes to the bar and pours herself just enough whiskey to clink glasses with her husband.*) To our finding each other again! (*She drinks her whiskey in one swallow, and looks at RUDY. He brings the glass to his lips, but stops suddenly as he spots the hundred and ten thousand on the desk.*)

RUDY. Ah! My one hundred and ten thousand! (*He goes to the desk, where he puts down his drink, and starts counting the money, using both hands.*)

MONIQUE. I haven't seen your Brazilian. You said he'd be coming around . . .

RUDY. I'll phone and spare him a trip. I'll meet him at his club tonight . . . (*Because of the pain, he's forced to count the money with one hand.*) Damn this hand! It hurts like blazes! . . . I'd better be sensible. Here, take half this drink! (*And he pours half into MONIQUE's glass.*) Tchin-Tchin! (*MONIQUE changes the conversation to avoid having to drink.*)

MONIQUE. You haven't finished counting the money!

RUDY. Oh, I'm a trusting soul!

MONIQUE. Then, put it in the drawer. Louise may come in!

RUDY. Right you are . . . (*He does so, turning his back to MONIQUE. She quickly empties her glass in the ice bucket and, as RUDY turns to her again, she brings the empty glass to her lips, making RUDY believe she's finished off the whiskey. He whistles.*) When you start to drink . . . !

MONIQUE. After the first drop, I forget how horrid it tastes! (*She puts down her glass.*)

RUDY. Well, since you've started, you might as well finish mine! My hand will thank you! Here! (*And he puts the drugged glass of whiskey in her hand! . . . MONIQUE is scared stiff.*) Well? Drink it!

MONIQUE. . . . Oh no! It's too much!

RUDY. Oh, come on! Drink my whiskey! I want to see

my Swiss Miss high on something other than goat milk! Come on! (*bullying her*) Drink it!

MONIQUE. Let me be! Why do you want to force me?

RUDY. Because it makes me laugh to see you high! Come on, make me laugh!

MONIQUE. No!

RUDY. Damn you, drink it! I want to laugh! (*He grabs his wife by the shoulders and forces her to drink. He laughs, enjoying her discomfort.*) If you could see the look on your face! It's irresistible! Swiss Miss swallows Scotch piss! (*MONIQUE rushes to pour herself a large glass of mineral water, which she drinks, hoping to weaken the effect of the sleeping pills.*) Oh! You're drowning the whiskey! My poor darling, you definitely don't know how to drink. But fortunately, you do know how to write checks! (*Laughing, he picks up his suitcase and topcoat and exits upstairs. LOUISE, quickly and quietly, comes in from the kitchen. She and MONIQUE lower their voices.*)

LOUISE. Did you drug the whiskey?

MONIQUE. Yes.

LOUISE. Did he drink it?

MONIQUE. No . . . I did!

LOUISE. Haaa! . . . What are you going to do?

MONIQUE. What can I do?

LOUISE. But you must do something! And before Corbeau arrives! (*They raise their voices as they hear RUDY coming.*) Where shall I serve lunch, madame?

MONIQUE. Why not on the terrace? It's a lovely day! (*RUDY enters.*)

RUDY. Good afternoon, Louise!

LOUISE. Good afternoon, monsieur. Did you have a good trip?

RUDY. Very. What are we having for lunch?

LOUISE. Pate, sliced filet, salad . . . with a bottle of your favorite Beaujolais, Saint-Amour.

RUDY. Marvelous!

MONIQUE. (*quickly*) Why not a glass before lunch? The doctor said no whiskey . . . but Saint-Amour . . . it's not really alcohol.

RUDY. Yes . . . a little wine couldn't hurt!

MONIQUE. (*her hopes rising*) Louise, uncork the bottle and bring it in here. I'll serve monsieur . . . (*LOUISE nods in accord and exits. Meanwhile, RUDY has gone to the mantelpiece to put his cigarillo in the ashtray. He is startled to see one already there . . . the one left by MICHEL*)

RUDY. What's this?

MONIQUE. (*terrified*) A cigarillo . . . one of your cigarillos.

RUDY. (*smells it, then:*) Who's been smoking it?

MONIQUE. I have!

RUDY. You're smoking now as well as drinking! My darling, you've discovered a great truth: people are loved not for their virtues but their vices! If you start taking drugs, I promise I'll love you forever! (*He lights another cigarillo and sits on the sofa. Meanwhile, LOUISE returns with the Beaujolais and gives the bottle to MONIQUE. The latter pours a glass and . . . plop! plop! plop! . . . three sleeping pills drop into the wine.*)

MONIQUE. (*casually*) Louise, give this glass of Beaujolais to monsieur! (*With trembling hand, LOUISE takes the glass and, trying to be natural, brings it to RUDY.*)

RUDY. Thank you, Louise. I hope things weren't too dull while I was away. What did you see on television? (*Comfortably installed on the sofa, RUDY unconsciously puts his hand between the cushions . . . the cushions where MONIQUE, in the first scene, hid the envelope from the prison in Fresnes.*) Yes? What did you see?

LOUISE. A detective story.

RUDY. Detective stories are a waste of time. You know from the beginning the villain will be caught. And that's not necessarily true. Is it? (*Suddenly, RUDY feels something strange between the cushions. While MONIQUE and LOUISE look on frightened, RUDY, using his fingertips, takes out the compromising envelope.*) ... Well, what's this? An envelope ... Empty! ... It's addressed to you, Louise! According to the postmark, you must have received it yesterday ... (*He looks at the back of the envelope. His face becomes set. Silence.*) Well! So yesterday you received a letter from ... ?

LOUISE. (*turning green*) ... No. I mean, a short note, that's all.

RUDY. The envelope is empty. I hope you haven't left the contents lying about?

LOUISE. (*betraying herself*) I burned it!

RUDY. (*pricking up his ears*) Burned it? ... It was a letter from your 'fiance,' wasn't it?

LOUISE. ... Yes!

RUDY. Is he well?

LOUISE. Very well.

RUDY. ... Is he still in the same place?

LOUISE. Still!

RUDY. And does he still like it there ... in Nigeria?

LOUISE. Yes.

RUDY. Well, since he still likes it ... in Nigeria ... he should stay there. When you write, don't forget to give him my best regards!

LOUISE. I will.

RUDY. Thank you! Here, burn the envelope, too! (*Holding the envelope by his fingertips, RUDY hands it to Louise, who rolls it into a ball before putting it in her apron pocket. Meanwhile, MONIQUE is beginning to feel the effects of the sleeping pills. She leans on the desk then drops into the chair with a cry. RUDY rushes to her side.*) Monique! Are you all right?

MONIQUE. (*shaking herself*) It's nothing . . . I'm a bit tired . . . I didn't sleep well last night.

RUDY. Here! Drink my wine! It will pick you up! (*He puts the drugged glass of wine in her hand and waits for her to drink.*) You're not drinking it, Monique. Why?

MONIQUE. . . . No . . . It's only a headache. (*He looks at MONIQUE and LOUISE, then speaks ironically.*)

RUDY. 'Only a headache.' There's something strange going on . . . something not quite right. Monique, drinking and refusing to drink. Louise, burning a letter and hiding the envelope between the cushions . . . (*suddenly*) Ah! I know what it is! Monique, you found Louise's letter and it upset you! That's it, isn't it? . . . Don't answer! I can tell by your face that you read the letter! So, the mystery is solved! Alas, my darling, I have a criminal for a brother. I wanted to keep the disgrace away from you. If Louise hadn't felt sorry for this scoundrel . . .

MONIQUE. Don't blame Louise for having a kind heart. Yes, I opened her mail, but it was by accident. I prefer to forget I ever read it. It doesn't concern me. We won't speak of it again. Ever!

RUDY. Thank you, Monique. Come let's drink to celebrate the end of this misunderstanding. We three are friends again! Yes, Louise?

LOUISE. (*relieved*) Oh yes, monsieur!

RUDY. (*diabolically*) Since my wife has a headache . . . here, Louise, you drink it! (*He puts the glass of drugged wine in her hand. LOUISE turns red.*)

LOUISE. (*stammering*) Heueueueuhhh!

Rudy. You don't want to? . . . I'll change the toast and we'll drink to my brother's health.

Louise. No!

Rudy. Why not? That isn't nice!

Louise. No . . . that is, I'm not thirsty!

Rudy. (*his face set*) I'm having no luck at all with this wine! No one wants to drink it. It must be poisoned!

Monique and Louise. (*forcing themselves to laugh*) Ha! Ha!

Rudy. . . . Or is it only drugged?

Monique. Oh, Rudy! Stop saying such things!

Rudy. Very well! Then prove to me this glass of Beaujolais is harmless! Drink it! Well? Who's going to volunteer? Or shall we toss a coin? (*MONIQUE and LOUISE are terrified. Suddenly, RUDY bursts out laughing and, with a grand theatrical gesture, pours the drugged wine into the ice bucket.*) You see, I really do trust people! (*MONIQUE and LOUISE look at each other and sigh with relief.*)

Louise. I must go and attend to lunch! (*She exits quickly into the kitchen. RUDY takes MONIQUE affectionately in his arms. She breaks away from him, nervously.*)

Rudy. Ashamed, my darling, because I have a brother in prison?

Monique. No . . . I told you, it doesn't matter! (*Reeling, she goes to sit . . . the sleeping pills are creeping up on her.*)

Rudy. I hope you don't think I'd let him rot in prison, without looking after him?

Monique. No . . .

Rudy. He doesn't get out until Christmas, but I arranged with the owner of the cafe across the street from the prison to deliver a food package every two weeks! On my word of honor!

DING DONG DEAD 61

MONIQUE. Let's not talk about it.

RUDY. I can tell by your manner that you don't believe me. Well, I'll prove it to you! (*He dials a telephone number.*)

MONIQUE. Who are you calling?

RUDY. Be patient for a second and you'll see I'm not the ogre you think I am! I'm not heartless! (*into the phone*) Hello? Hello? Cafe Mafioso? . . . Is Franco there? . . . Hello, Franco? This is Rudy Popesco. (*LOUISE has come into the room. She stands and listens.*) How's business? . . . No, I don't want to become your partner! I called because I want my brother to get an extra food package this week . . . I'm in a generous mood . . . (*suddenly bewildered*) What? . . . No! You're joking! . . . Paroled? When? . . . What? This morning? I'll be damned! . . . No, I haven't seen him. He didn't come to the house! . . . Thanks, Franco. Thanks for the information. (*He hangs up angrily, but then turns to MONIQUE and LOUISE and speaks all too sweetly. The women are in a state.*) Well, my angels, been playing games, have you? But you're out of luck! . . . I suspected something was wrong the minute I set foot in here! You were both too sweet to me! (*He laughs wickedly.*) It wasn't normal! (*Suddenly, his face turns evil as he advances on them. Terrified, MONIQUE and LOUISE put their arms around each other.*) Orphans of the storm! How touching! . . . Are you going to tell me what happened? . . . No? Then I'll tell you. Michel gets out of prison. He comes here. He tells you everything. You console him. You hide him and try to keep it from me . . . I'm sorry to have to do this, but we three are going to spend a very ugly fifteen minutes! And 'brave' little Michel is not here to defend you! . . . Ah! I know where he's hiding! At the bottom of the garden, next to the well, in his own little nook! He dug a hole in the ivy and covered his face with a geranium! Well, I just might pluck the flower . . . and, at the same time, split his skull open! (*He takes out a revolver from his pocket.*) And then shoot him to make sure! (*MONIQUE cries out in fear.*)

MONIQUE. No! You wouldn't do that . . .

LOUISE. Oh, monsieur, have pity! No! Michel! Michel! Michel! (*She rushes to the terrace and disappears into the garden, still shouting.*)

RUDY. So I was right. Michel is here! That little coward knows too much about me . . . and insults me by looking like me! It's time I got rid of him! (*He starts for the terrace, holding the gun . . . but MONIQUE blocks his path.*) Get out of my way! (*He pushes her back towards the sofa.*)

MONIQUE. (*reeling, almost sleepwalking*) No! I won't let you kill your brother!

RUDY. Why? (*suddenly*) Ooooh! You're plotting! You want to use Michel, is that it? Use him because he looks like me?

MONIQUE. No! (*The sleeping pills are getting the better of her. She grabs the arm of the sofa to keep from falling.*)

RUDY. What's the matter? You look sick. It couldn't, by any chance, be the whiskey . . . the whiskey I made you drink . . . was drugged?

MONIQUE. (*in a whisper*) No . . .

RUDY. Liar! When you plot a crime, make sure you can see it through to the end, otherwise it can boomerang! There are three bullets in this gun. One is marked for my brother! The second is for Louise, if she opens her mouth! And the third, my darling, is for you, if you don't sign over your entire fortune to me! (*He heads for the terrace. With a last burst of energy, MONIQUE grabs his wounded hand, making him pivot.*) Ouch! My hand! You bitch!

(*They struggle. You can't tell who has the upperhand. Suddenly, a shot rings out . . . Suspense! MONIQUE, ashen, frees herself from RUDY . . . as he slowly turns towards us. The gun, which is turned towards him, drops from his hand. He looks at his mortal wound incredulously, then raises his eyes to his wife . . . LOUISE rushes in from the terrace.*)

LOUISE. I heard a shot!
MONIQUE. We were struggling . . . the gun went off . . . (*The death rattle. RUDY's knees buckle under and he falls in the middle of the room . . . dead . . . his arms crossed. In a whisper:*) The sleeping pills . . . Louise, the room's turning . . . I feel sick . . . (*She starts to fall.*)
LOUISE. (*catching and supporting her*) Madame! (*Another dizzy spell. LOUISE helps MONIQUE stretch out on the sofa, then rushes to the terrace, shouting:*) Michel! . . . Micheeeel! . . . Come quickly! There are complications! Complications! (*She disappears into the garden. MONIQUE is sound asleep.*)

BLACKOUT

CURTAIN

ACT TWO

Scene 1

The same, one hour later. MONIQUE, still asleep from the effect of the opiate, is stretched out on the sofa. LOUISE enters from the kitchen. She looks at MONIQUE and tries to wake her. She raises MONIQUE's head and makes her drink a glass of water. MONIQUE regains consciousness.

MONIQUE. Oh! . . . My head! . . . What happened? . . . What am I doing lying here?

LOUISE. The sleeping pills, madame . . . not to mention the shock!

MONIQUE. (*growing more aware*) Shock? What shock? . . . Ooooooh, my God! Rudy! I killed him!

LOUISE. No, you didn't kill him, madame; it was an accident! Self-defense. He got the bullet instead of you. That's all . . .

MONIQUE. (*suddenly*) But . . . the body? What are we going to do with the body?

LOUISE. That's already been taken care of, madame!

MONIQUE. Oh?

LOUISE. . . . The well at the bottom of the garden is very deep. If you drop a pebble, you can't hear it fall! While you were sleeping, Michel and I dragged out the body and pushed it over into the well. As a precaution, Michel emptied two wheelbarrow loads of dirt on top!

MONIQUE. (*appalled*) Oooooh!

LOUISE. Madame is shocked?

MONIQUE. Yes . . .

LOUISE. But spared the bother of what to do with the

body. For this additional service, there will be an additional charge of one hundred thousand francs!

MONIQUE. (*stunned*) . . . What logic!

LOUISE. I'm like you in that respect, madame. You saw Michel's resemblence and plotted your divorce. I saw the checkbook and plotted my future!

MONIQUE. It's a nightmare . . .

LOUISE. (*looking at her wristwatch*) It's a quarter to two, madame.

MONIQUE. Yes? What of it?

LOUISE. Corbeau! He'll be here at two! You must get up!

MONIQUE. Oh! But there's no reason to go through with the plan now! . . . I must give up this idea of Rudy's 'double.'

LOUISE. Why give it up?

MONIQUE. (*logically*) Since Rudy is dead . . . I am a widow!

LOUISE. (*with a laugh*) A widow! Yes, you are a widow! But if you tell how your husband died, you'll have a problem . . . and end your days in prison!

MONIQUE. . . . But you just said it was self-defense!

LOUISE. Yes, I did! . . . But what will the police say? 'Self-defense? Prove it! Do you have any witnesses?'

MONIQUE. Yes! . . . You!

LOUISE. Me? You can't be serious!

MONIQUE. What?

LOUISE. (*realistically*) Michel and I can't take risks! We can't be involved in murder! Even if it's accidental! Michel came out of prison this morning. How would it look? No! No! I gave it a lot of thought while madame was sleeping. We must go through with your plan. You'll get the signed divorce papers! And we'll get our money! And if the body is not discovered immediately, fine! You can say Rudy talked of going to South America. And if the body is found, you can tell the police of the Corsican bandit who threatened to kill him in Marseilles!

MONIQUE. Lies, lies, you want me to drown in a sea of lies!

LOUISE. No, madame! I want to protect you! And I want to protect Michel! After tonight, we three can leave this house rich and free and forever.

MONIQUE. (*weakening*) Yes. Perhaps you're right . . . What do we have to do now?

LOUISE. Nothing . . . since nothing has changed! Corbeau will be here in a few minutes! Michel will double for Rudy!

MONIQUE. Yes, you're right, we must go on! It's our only hope. (*LOUISE helps MONIQUE up.*)

LOUISE. A cup of black coffee?

MONIQUE. Yes, I think so. (*A noise from the kitchen . . . MONIQUE is frightened.*)

LOUISE. Don't be afraid, madame, it's Michel! (*MICHEL enters. He is in his shirtsleeves, with his glasses on his nose, and carrying a large sheet of paper. LOUISE crosses to him.*) Well?

MICHEL. I did it, Louise.

MONIQUE. Did what?

LOUISE. I asked Michel to keep practising the signature . . . Let me see . . . (*MICHEL hands the paper to LOUISE, who studies it, before passing it to MONIQUE.*) What do you think?

MONIQUE. Better. Much better.

MICHEL. Are you pleased with me, Loulou?

LOUISE. Yes. And madame has 'volunteered' to give us a bonus!

MICHEL. Ooooh! How much does that make? I can't keep up!

LOUISE. You don't have to. I'm counting. (*looking at her watch*) Ten minutes to two! Time to brush up once more before Corbeau arrives. I'll get the coffee. (*She exits into the kitchen. MICHEL puts on the jacket to his suit, which suddenly seems to fit him better.*)

(*NOTE: Use two identical jackets for the actor, this one fitting him well.*)

MICHEL. It's getting exciting! I can feel the adrenalin flowing! . . . It gives me confidence!

MONIQUE. That's good.

MICHEL. Look! Even Rudy's jacket fits better!

MONIQUE. Yes, it does seem to.

MICHEL. It must! I'm not losing this chance of a lifetime!

MONIQUE. You won't.

MICHEL. I feel sure I can imitate Rudy's signature perfectly now! You'll see! Perfectly! (*He takes a clean sheet of paper, picks up the pen and, with a flourish, writes RUDY's name. He shows it to MONIQUE.*)

MONIQUE. (*whistling*) Extraordinary!

MICHEL. Rudy's death has set me free of him! I have become Rudy! (*LOUISE enters with the coffee on a tray, which she puts on the bar.*)

MONIQUE. Louise, look at this signature. Even I would be fooled!

LOUISE. (*to MICHEL*) Since you've become such an expert, my little penman, I can see I'm going to have to keep an eye on you!

MICHEL. Oooooh, Loulou, I'd never forge your name! (*Laughing, she hugs MICHEL.*)

MONIQUE. Corbeau shouldn't be much longer.
MICHEL. (*suddenly*) . . . Then give us the third check!
MONIQUE. What!
MICHEL. There, you see, just like Rudy!
MONIQUE. The check is already made out. (*She tears it out of her checkbook and gives it to MICHEL. Suddenly, the sound of a car parking. MICHEL pockets the check.*) It's Corbeau! (*She takes up a position to greet him.*)
LOUISE. (*to MICHEL*) Behind the desk! Quickly!
MICHEL. I'm going to amaze you, Loulou! (*He sits behind the desk and lights a cigarillo. He strikes a pose and holds it.*)
MONIQUE. (*to both, whispering*) . . . God be with us! . . . (*louder*) Oh, my God! Take off your glasses!

(*MICHEL obeys. CORBEAU enters.*)

CORBEAU. Ah, my friends, here we are again! My dear Rudy, how are you feeling now?
MICHEL. Marvelous! I must apologize for my behaviour this morning . . . but I was rather 'sloshed.' But now that I've had a nap, I'm 'fresh as a daisy!'
CORBEAU. Splendid! Splendid!
MONIQUE. Won't you sit down? (*CORBEAU crosses to the sofa, searching through his briefcase.*)
CORBEAU. . . . First, Rudy, I phoned my bank. Everything's fine! A check from the sale of your shares has been deposited to my account! Let me return your note. (*As he crosses towards 'RUDY,' MONIQUE bars his way. She takes the note and, with a big smile, tears it up.*)
MICHEL. Thank you, my darling! Come on, let's get on with the proceedings! Time is money!

MONIQUE. Indeed it is! . . . Rudy, do you still want the divorce?
MICHEL. Yes!
MONIQUE. No regrets?
MICHEL. None! I've had enough of the joys of marriage! I won't miss a single one of our quarrels! . . . I wish you well in Switzerland! . . . Is that clear enough?
MONIQUE. (*with a smile*) Oh yes, Rudy! I knew you wouldn't change your mind!
CORBEAU. I am delighted for you! And for me! And that it's all so friendly! (*He takes out the papers from his briefcase and puts them in order on his knees.*) I brought the papers for you to sign so we can start judicial proceedings . . . I'll spare you the details. But you can trust me, it's my profession! . . . As I have already explained to your wife, Rudy, I'll turn these papers over to a friend, a lawyer who specializes in divorce . . .
RUDY. Yes, yes, of course! Everyone specializes these days!
CORBEAU. Yes, Rudy. But the law is a labyrinth and no client would escape if there wasn't a specialist. He'd smother in the red tape! . . . But divorce lawyers know how to play the Napoleonic Code like a toreador does a bull! Sidestep, sidestep . . . then, whack! Between the eyes! Divorce granted!

(*During the above, MONIQUE is thunderstruck when she sees MICHEL has forgotten to put the dressing on his hand! Desperately, she pantomines to LOUISE. She panics. So does MICHEL, who becomes a frightened little man again . . . Suddenly, LOUISE remembers the adhesive plaster in the drawer. She quickly takes it out and cuts off a piece with the scissors. She puts the plaster on the palm of MICHEL's left hand . . . just in time! . . . for CORBEAU, who has collated the papers, rises, crosses to the desk, and puts them under MICHEL's nose.*)

CORBEAU. (*continued*) Here you are, my friend.

MICHEL. Oh! Thank you! (*Without hesitating, he starts to sign the papers.*)

MONIQUE. (*a diversionary tactic*) Would you care for a cup of coffee, dear Monsieur Corbeau?

CORBEAU. No, thank you!

MONIQUE. While Rudy is signing, I'll make out a check for your fee . . .

CORBEAU. (*pricking up his ears*) I have the bill right here! (*He takes the bill from his wallet. It's for more than MONIQUE expected. She looks questioningly at him.*) Er . . . You wanted it done quickly . . . for which there's a small supplement . . . for the typist, who I kept during her lunch hour . . .

MONIQUE. Of course! It's quite legitimate! I rushed you! Rudy made up his mind quickly . . .

CORBEAU. Yes, exactly, madame . . . your husband's haste rather surprises me. (*He crosses slowly to MICHEL.*) Rudy, I've always known you to be an impetuous man, but never with a decision of this importance! It's not like you. A divorce? It's more like a transformation on your part! . . . Do you know what I think? You're no longer the same man! . . . Isn't that funny? (*MICHEL starts to panic. Suddenly:*) Rudy . . . you have no dressing on your hand.

MICHEL. No. It was only a minor cut. (*With a bit more assurance, he holds up his hand with the adhesive plaster.*) All I need is this.

CORBEAU. (*baffled*) My, but you heal quickly!

MICHEL. Yes . . .

(*Nevertheless, CORBEAU has a flea in his ear. He scrutinizes 'RUDY's signature. Our three accomplices have some anxious moments. MICHEL grabs a cup of coffee and drinks it quickly.*)

CORBEAU. Coffee is bad for the heart, Rudy! And for the nerves! I never touch it. In my profession you need to keep a cool head and a sure eye. You know, in all the years I've been drawing up legal documents, I can honestly say I've never once been taken in!

MONIQUE. Congratulations!

CORBEAU. Besides coffee can shorten your life! It's true! . . . here, look at my life line! (*He opens his hand and shows it to MONIQUE.*) I'll live to be ninety-five at least!

MONIQUE. You will indeed! (*Laughing, CORBEAU opens MONIQUE's hand and studies it.*)

CORBEAU. Oh, you too have a marvelous life line, madame! And this line . . . extraordinary! You have a head on your shoulders and a will to match. You're stronger than you let people believe, madame!

MONIQUE. Really? (*With authority, he opens LOUISE's hand.*)

CORBEAU. Oh, dear, oh, dear!

LOUISE. What is it?

CORBEAU. Where's your line for luck? . . . You're going to have trouble, and lots of it!

LOUISE. Ohhh! (*CORBEAU takes MICHEL's "wounded" hand and holds it with an iron grip. He separates the fingers though MICHEL tries hard to prevent it.*)

CORBEAU. . . . As for you, my dear Rudy . . . Yes . . . Yes . . . Shall I tell you everything I see? Shall I? (*He rips off the adhesive plaster, discovering the hand is indeed without a cut.*) I see only one thing: you're not

Rudy! . . . You must be his brother. He told me about you, about the resemblance! Yes, it's astonishing!

MICHEL. Yes, isn't it?

CORBEAU. What's your name?

MICHEL. . . . Michel!

CORBEAU. Thanks. (*then suddenly, icily*) You three must think I'm stupid! (*He picks up the divorce papers and tears them in four.*) Now you know I'm not! (*He throws the pieces in MICHEL's face. MICHEL crosses to the desk, where he breaks down in despair.*)

MICHEL. I knew this would happen . . . I knew it . . .

CORBEAU. (*turning to MONIQUE*) I'll give you thirty seconds to justify yourself madame.

MONIQUE. (*with tears in her eyes*) My husband is a monster, you know it! He wanted to steal my fortune . . . kill me. I tried to trick him . . . (*She throws herself on the sofa and covers her face with her hands, crying.*)

CORBEAU. (*turning to LOUISE*) And you, mademoiselle? What justification can you give me?

LOUISE. I love Michel! We want to marry . . . and live abroad! (*And she bursts into tears. CORBEAU looks from LOUISE to MONIQUE to MICHEL . . . all three in tears.*)

CORBEAU. How touching! Shall I take out my handkerchief and cry, too? (*a pause*) . . . Oh, I know Rudy is a scoundrel! . . . Yes, I understand why you tried to trick him by this extraordinary resemblance to his brother! Yes, extraordinary! It would tempt the devil! But . . . but . . . (*a long pause*) What should I do? What is right under the circumstances? (*MONIQUE, LOUISE and MICHEL look up, worried and waiting for his decision. They are a truly pitiable trio.*) Very well. (*to MICHEL and LOUISE*) If you and the maid promise to leave France immediately, I'll forget your involvment in the attempt at fraud.

MICHEL. Yes, we'll go! I swear!
LOUISE. Yes! Now! At once!
MICHEL. (*growing more and more excited*) Oh, thank you, Monsieur Corbeau! You're kind! Thank you! I'm so happy . . . look, I'm trembling with joy! . . . At first, I didn't want to do it, but they insisted! One thing led to another! . . . Poor Rudy! Who could have guessed how it would turn out! (*CORBEAU pricks up his ears. MONIQUE and LOUISE listen to MICHEL with growing concern.*) But he deserved it! All his life Rudy dominated me. It had to end one day! (*CORBEAU knits his brow. MONIQUE and LOUISE panic. MICHEL gets in deeper and deeper.*) And I'll tell you another thing: I hated Rudy! He was my brother, sure, but he was not a good brother, he was bad . . .
CORBEAU. Excuse me, but you're speaking of him in a strange way. 'Poor Rudy . . . he was my brother . . . he was bad.' It sounds like you never expect to see him again! . . . What trick have you played on him? (*MICHEL realizes his blunder, at last, and remains silent.*)
MONIQUE. (*distraught*) . . . What he means is that Rudy . . . has changed . . . that is, he's going to change . . . for the better . . . (*She trails off.*)
CORBEAU. But where is he? He left Marseilles. Have you seen him since he got back? . . . Or did you get rid of him? Spirit him out of the house? But if so, how? I know Rudy. He's too clever to be duped! Come on, tell me, where is Rudy? (*silence*) What did you do to get him out of the way before I arrived? (*laughing*) You haven't killed him, have you?
MICHEL. (*crying out*) Yes!
CORBEAU. What?
MICHEL. But it was an accident!
MONIQUE. (*confessing*) He threatened me with a gun! We struggled! The gun went off! He fell, here, in the

middle of the room, dead!

CORBEAU. (*ashen*) Dead! But what have you done with his body?

LOUISE. . . . We threw it down the well!

CORBEAU. Mother of God! (*He takes the news like a punch in the stomach. He stands there with an open mouth, then sits.*) . . . To close my eyes to fraud is one thing . . . but to murder . . . never! No! I must call the police! At once! (*He crosses to the phone and picks up the receiver. Suddenly, LOUISE takes out RUDY's revolver from her apron pocket and points it at CORBEAU.*)

LOUISE. Put down that telephone! (*CORBEAU, surprised and terrified, obeys.*) Put your hands up! All of you!

MONIQUE. All of us? But . . .

LOUISE. Do as I say or I shoot! (*MONIQUE and CORBEAU raise their hands.*) You, too, Michel!

MICHEL. But Loulou . . .

LOUISE. There's no more Loulou! Put up your hands! (*MICHEL obeys.*) Step back. All of you, against the staircase. Go on, move! (*Frightened, CORBEAU, MONIQUE and MICHEL group together, as LOUISE holds the gun pointed at them.*)

MONIQUE. Louise, don't be a fool!

LOUISE. (*contemptuously*) When have I ever been? But what a fool you have been, and from the very first day! Don't you understand, I planned it all! (*indicating MICHEL*) I pulled this puppet by the strings . . . and I led you around by the nose! I put the letter from the prison in your hands! I told you about the two brothers looking alike! And you never suspected a thing! I led you exactly where I wanted . . . that is, to your checkbook!

MICHEL. Oh! No!

LOUISE. Oh! Yes! . . . Come on, you idiot, hand over the checks in your pocket! And be quick about it! (*MICHEL, with trembling hands, throws the checks on the desk. She pockets them.*) And you, madame, make out the last installment! And don't forget to include my one hundred thousand bonus! (*MONIQUE sits and writes the check.*) Made payabe 'to bearer,' of course! And don't try to stop payment! If you do, I'll tell the police to look in the well and see what they can find down there! (*LOUISE takes the check with a triumphant smile. MONIQUE rises and takes her place again between the two men.*) Thank you, madame! . . . You see, I'm not even looking at the amount. I trust you! (*She pockets the check.*) As for you, Monsieur Corbeau, your employees know where you are so, like it or not, you are now involved in this crime, too! Don't anybody move! I hope you left your key in the car, Monsieur Corbeau?

CORBEAU. Yes, but . . . You're behaving like a fool! I'm a sworn official! If I go to the police and declare, on my honor, that you instigated this . . . that you are even responsible for Rudy's death . . . you will be caught wherever you go . . . by Interpol! (*He takes two steps towards her.*)

MONIQUE. Be careful!

LOUISE. You don't frighten me!

CORBEAU. You can't escape. (*She backs away as CORBEAU continues towards her.*)

LOUISE. Stay where you are!

CORBEAU. Give me that gun!

LOUISE. Don't move!

CORBEAU. Give it to me!

LOUISE. No!

CORBEAU. Bitch!

LOUISE. Oh! You asked for it! (*He takes another step towards her. She loses her head and fires. The bullet hits CORBEAU in the heart. He drops to the floor . . . dead.*)

MICHEL. . . . And he thought he'd live to be ninety-five!

MONIQUE. (*in a whisper*) We're lost . . .

LOUISE. Lost? On the contrary, I saved you! I eliminated the one man who could expose us! You should write me another check!

MONIQUE. Money! Money! Can't you think of anything but money?

MICHEL. What's going to happen to us?

LOUISE. Nothing! We're free! We'll go our separate ways!

MONIQUE. You're going to let us go? You're not going to kill us, too?

LOUISE. Definitely not you, madame! I need you alive! Dead your bank account will be blocked!

MONIQUE. . . . And what are we going to do with Corbeau's body?

LOUISE. Don't bother your head about it, madame! Down the well!

MICHEL. Again!

LOUISE. Be quiet! This is all your fault! Babbling, babbling, never knowing when to stop! You idiot, get rid of 'that!' (*She indicates the body. MICHEL, humiliated, terrified, drags the body towards the terrace.*)

MICHEL. (*his face contorted*) Two bodies in one afternoon! And I'm only out of prison since this morning! (*He exits, dragging the body.*)

MONIQUE. Horrible . . . it's horrible!

LOUISE. Bah! Two dirty bastards! Good riddance! I'm

going to drive Corbeau's car back to Paris. I'll leave it outside his office! Don't worry, nobody will see me! Goodbye, madame.

MONIQUE. Forever?

LOUISE. . . . Forever. Say goodbye to Michel for me, too! Partings are such sweet pleasure!

MONIQUE. What about your things?

LOUISE. I'm packed, ready to go, with only your checks to remember you by . . . (*Still talking, she exits into the kitchen. Suddenly, MONIQUE rushes quietly up to the kitchen door and turns the key in the lock. LOUISE is trapped inside! In a state of nerves, MONIQUE rushes to the phone and dials.*)

MONIQUE. (*into phone*) Hello? Police Emergency? (*panting*) I need help! Please! At once! . . . Madame Popesco! . . . *Madame Rudy Popesco!* . . . I can't explain now! There's no time! Listen to me, I'm in danger! I'm going into the woods . . .

LOUISE. (*off-stage*) The door is locked! Madame! Did you lock the door? . . . Open it! Open it! . . . If you're playing games . . . !

MONIQUE. (*into phone*) Tell the Chief Inspector! He knows me! . . . *Popesco!* There have been two crimes committed here . . . two horrible crimes . . .

LOUISE. (*off-stage*) Open the door! Open it, I tell you!

MONIQUE. (*into phone*) I'll take the path to the old chateau . . . *The old chateau!* Hurry! Oh, please hurry! (*LOUISE is shouting behind the kitchen door. Terrified, MONIQUE quickly puts down the receiver. She rushes out and disappears beyond the terrace.*)

BLACKOUT

Scene 2

The same, one hour later. A police siren breaks the silence. A car screeches to a halt. Car doors slam. Suddenly, TWO POLICEMEN with guns invade the room. The 1ST POLICEMAN goes upstairs and disappears. The 2ND POLICEMAN goes into the kitchen.

MONIQUE and the CHIEF INSPECTOR enter. He is middle-aged, with an open manner and sympathetic face. He must inspire confidence, a feeling of security. He holds MONIQUE gently by the arm. She has been crying again . . .

The 2ND POLICEMAN re-enters from the kitchen.

INSPECTOR. (*to the POLICEMAN*) Search the house from top to bottom . . .

2ND POLICEMAN. Yes, Inspector. (*He exits.*)

INSPECTOR. (*to MONIQUE*) Come inside! You're in your own home, madame! And I am with you. You have nothing to fear.

MONIQUE. That's true!

INSPECTOR. Please . . . sit down . . .

MONIQUE. Thank you, Inspector.

INSPECTOR. I'm only doing my duty. I have your story quite clear. That is why, if you wish, I'd like to examine the facts more closely . . .

MONIQUE. I was so upset . . . terrified . . . and then I remembered meeting you, Inspector . . .

INSPECTOR. Yes, I remember that night. Your husband was drunk and smashed his car. I formed a bad impression of Monsieur Popesco at the time and, from what you tell me now, I wasn't wrong. Your husband is a fortune hunter. You're his victim. These things happen . . .

(*TWO POLICEMEN enter.*)

1st Policeman. The house is empty . . .

2nd Policeman. Nobody here!

Inspector. (*to 1ST POLICEMAN*) Look outside. Cover the entire property . . . (*1ST POLICEMAN exits. To 2ND POLICEMAN:*) Tell me, is Alfred in the car, keeping in radio contact with the station?

2nd Policeman. Yes, Inspector.

Inspector. Good. As soon as he gets any of the information I asked for, let me know. And give the P. J. in Paris this telephone number so they can contact me directly . . . (*2ND POLICEMAN exits. To MONIQUE:*) I'm checking out the facts you have given me.

Monique. Thank you, Inspector. Thank you with all my heart. (*He takes out her statement from his pocket.*)

Inspector. . . . Now I want to go over the essential points of your statement before you sign it. (*He consults the papers.*) You say your husband, Rudy, mistreated you . . . that you gave him considerable sums of money . . .

Monique. Yes.

Inspector. Unfortunately, that's a matter between husband and wife, not for the police. The first important point of interest to us is your husband's brother, Michel. You say he got out of prison this morning.

Monique. Yes, from Fresnes. And they look as alike as two drops of water!

Inspector. Right. And you admit, madame, that aided and abetted by your maid, Louise, you taught Michel how to impersonate your husband . . . the aim being a friendly divorce, with Michel signing the necessary papers in the presence of a Monsieur Corbeau, Champs-Elysees, Paris. That is fraud, madame . . . punishable under the law.

MONIQUE. . . . Yes, I know! . . . But I could see no other way of freeing myself of that despicable man!

INSPECTOR. No doubt the judge will take that into consideration . . . (*consulting his papers*) . . . Now, madame, we come to your husband's murder.

MONIQUE. It was an accident! He threatened me . . . we struggled . . . the gun went off, I don't know how!

INSPECTOR. Right. And to cover up the accident, Michel, with the assistance of Louise, threw your husband's body down the well.

MONIQUE. Yes!

INSPECTOR. . . . And in this same well, we will also find the body of Monsieur Corbeau, shot to death by Louise!

MONIQUE. (*sobbing*) Yes! My God! My God!

(*1ST POLICEMAN enters.*)

1ST POLICEMAN. There's no one out there, Inspector.

INSPECTOR. Have you looked down the well?

1ST POLICEMAN. The well, Inspector?

INSPECTOR. At the bottom of the garden! Do it quickly! (*1ST POLICEMAN exits by the terrace.*) . . . And so, madame, after this series of horrible events, you fled the house, hopefully to get in touch with me! (*MONIQUE nods, too overwhelmed to speak.*) If what you tell me is accurate, your brother-in-law and Louise cannot have gotten far! My men will pick them up. Here . . . sign your statement. (*MONIQUE signs and is suddenly relieved and confident.*)

MONIQUE. Oh, thank you, Inspector!

INSPECTOR. Relax now . . . (*2ND POLICEMAN enters. He hands the INSPECTOR a message and exits. The INSPECTOR reads it and looks baffled.*)

MONIQUE. What is it?

INSPECTOR. There's news already . . . but it's puzzling. The P. J. has no record of a Michel Popesco!

MONIQUE. But . . . in Fresnes?

INSPECTOR. The warden in Fresnes reports he has never had a prisoner by that name!

MONIQUE. It's not possible! What about the other prisons around Paris?

INSPECTOR. They have checked everywhere! The name Michel Popesco is not known to the P. J.!

MONIQUE. But why would Michel tell me he came out of prison if it's not true?

INSPECTOR. (*puzzled*) Yes, why? (*2ND POLICEMAN enters (and exits) with another message for the INSPECTOR, who reads it.*) More news: there has been no passenger by the name of Rudy Popesco on any airline in the past forty-eight hours. Are you sure, madame, that your husband went to Marseilles?

MONIQUE. Yes! He phoned me from Marseilles! I spoke with the district operator at Bouches-du-Rhone. She made the connection.

INSPECTOR. (*startled*) What?! Then you were tricked, madame. A district operator is no longer needed for Marseilles. The system has been completely automated!

MONIQUE. (*flabbergasted*) Yes! That's true! What does this mean? (*2ND POLICEMAN enters (and exits) with a third message for the INSPECTOR.*)

INSPECTOR. (*commenting on the message*) There is no Corbeau in Certified Legal Documents on the Champs-Elysees . . . nor in any other part of Paris. (*Telephone rings.*) That must be for me! (*He picks up the receiver.*) Hello? Yes? . . . The P. J.? Inspector Murzeau speaking . . . Ah, it's you, Jacques! How are you? (*He laughs.*) Tell me, did you get the information I wanted from the

Bureau of Records? . . . Oh? . . . Oh? (*He whistles.*) Well! What do you know? Thanks, Jacques. My best to the gang. (*He hangs up and looks at MONIQUE in dismay.*)

MONIQUE. What did he say?

INSPECTOR. According to the Bureau of Records, your husband, Rudy Popesco, never had a brother!

MONIQUE. (*repeats like a somnambulist*) . . . never had a brother?

(*1ST POLICEMAN enters, carrying a flashlight.*)

1ST POLICEMAN. Inspector, there is nothing in the well! The water is as clear as crystal. You can see right down to the bottom! (*On a gesture from the INSPECTOR, the 1ST POLICEMAN exits.*)

INSPECTOR. Madame, don't you think it would be advisable if you went over your statement again?

MONIQUE. (*her face distorted*) It's not possible! I'm losing my mind!

INSPECTOR. (*gently*) The facts . . . let's go over the facts . . . (*Point by point he goes over MONIQUE's statement, growing more and more incredulous.*) You say a letter arrived from Fresnes prison . . . the letter which has been burned. It was addressed to your maid . . . and there's no maid here. You have a brother-in-law . . . who doesn't exist. You tell me of a trip your husband made to Marseilles . . . where he hasn't been! Of Corbeau, who has no address, no practise. And, to top it all, of two bodies in a well . . . two bodies which have dissolved in crystal clear water! Don't you think you should make a new statement, madame?

MONIQUE. But I swear to you . . .

INSPECTOR. (*gently*) Are you well, madame? Are you subject to . . . hallucinations?

Monique. Everything I told you is true! True! True!
Inspector. I'm sorry, everything is false! False! False!
Monique. No! (*crying out*) I'm not crazy! I'm not!
Inspector. (*grumbling*) It's what they all say in these cases!
Monique. I must stay calm, calm, calm . . . calm!

(*2ND POLICEMAN enters.*)

2nd Policeman. A man outside insists on seeing you, Inspector!
Inspector. Who is he?
2nd Policeman. Monsieur Rudy Popesco!
Monique. No!
Inspector. Please, madame! . . . Let him come in. (*2ND POLICEMAN exits. There is a silence. RUDY appears on the terrace. He pretends to be greatly astonished.*)
Rudy. What's happening? Why are the police here, my darling? (*He recognizes the INSPECTOR*) . . . Why, it's you, Inspector! What a surprise! But why are you here?
Inspector. (*embarrassed*) Er . . . Monsieur Popesco . . . how are you? (*to MONIQUE*) Well . . . your husband is alive!
Monique. Alive!
Rudy. Yes, my darling, alive and well . . . happily! But why do you look surprised?
Monique. You were lying here . . . in the middle of the room . . . dead!
Rudy. (*acting distraught*) Me? Oh! Your mind is straying again! (*to the INSPECTOR*) . . . Tell me, Inspector, what's going on? Please! I don't understand!

INSPECTOR. Neither do I! Monsieur Popesco, your wife has told me a story . . . a rather bizarre story, with two dead bodies . . .

RUDY. Two?

INSPECTOR. . . . based on the fact you have a brother, who . . .

RUDY. (*interrupting; nonplussed*) What? . . . But I have no brother!

INSPECTOR. I know! I just found out. And that isn't all. Do you know a Monsieur Corbeau, who frequents the gaming tables?

RUDY. (*explicitly*) No! I do not know any Corbeau and I have never set foot in a gambling casino!

MONIQUE. (*crying out*) Oh! That's a lie! It's a conspiracy! Yes, that's what it is . . . a conspiracy against me! You . . . you . . . you . . . (*Her brain is spinning. She feels dizzy and falls on the sofa. RUDY rushes to her side.*)

RUDY. My love . . . my angel! . . . It's all right, Inspector, I know what to do . . . (*He holds a small bottle under her nose. She breathes in and the fumes calm her.*)

INSPECTOR. Have you consulted a doctor?

RUDY. (*speaking low*) We've seen a dozen! I'm expecting Professor Falkenhausen this afternoon. He's the eminent psychiatrist. My wife is his patient now. He comes to see her often . . .

INSPECTOR. Your wife spoke of a maid by the name of Louise . . .

RUDY. Louise? She left our service two months ago! My wife's seizures frightened her! . . . I hired a nurse. Haven't you seen her?

INSPECTOR. We haven't seen anyone. The house is empty!

RUDY. That's strange!

DING DONG DEAD

(*Suddenly, the voices of the TWO POLICEMEN are heard off-stage, arguing with LOUISE.*)

LOUISE. (*off-stage*) Will you let me pass! . . . I work here! My papers? No, I will not show you my papers! . . . We'll see about that! . . . One word from me to the President of the Red Cross and you two men . . . (*And suddenly SIMONE (formerly LOUISE) enters from the terrace. She is wearing a cape over a plain blue dress and carries a nurse's bag. Her hair is in a bun and, with no make-up, she looks as dry as a stick.*) Monsieur, what is the meaning of this?

RUDY. Please! My wife had another attack! . . . She called the Police!

MONIQUE. Louise!

SIMONE. Oh! Madame! I shouldn't have left you! You'll feel better after your medication!

MONIQUE. (*to the INSPECTOR*) It's Louise! . . . It's Louise!

SIMONE. Why does she call me 'Louise?'

RUDY. Inspector, this is Simone Marsan, a registered nurse.

MONIQUE. That's a lie! Her name is Louise! She's our maid!

INSPECTOR. (*to SIMONE*) Excuse me, but for my report, I shall have to see your identification.

SIMONE. (*acting annoyed*) You, too? Well . . . if it's necessary . . . (*She plunges her hand inside her dress, takes out her wallet, from which she extracts her identity card and passes it under the INSPECTOR's nose with disdain.*) Is this what you want?

RUDY. Where have you been?

SIMONE. Is that a reproach, monsieur? I gave madame a sedative before I left the house! What is it this time?

RUDY. . . . A thriller . . . with two dead bodies!

SIMONE. I'm not surprised! I told monsieur long ago to get rid of those murder mysteries she devours! (*INSPECTOR returns the identity card to SIMONE.*)

MONIQUE. (*crying out*) It's a lie! A lie! (*to SIMONE*) Bitch! Bitch!

SIMONE. If you start insulting me again, madame, like you did last week, I shall be forced to give you one of those injections you don't like!

(*Sound of a car parking in the driveway. RUDY rushes to the terrace.*)

RUDY. It's Professor Falkenhausen!
INSPECTOR. (*with a gesture to his men off-stage*) Let him in!
SIMONE. What a relief!
RUDY. Ah! Professor! Come in! Come in!

(*MAX (formerly CORBEAU) enters. He is elegantly dressed, wears eyeglasses and carries a doctor's bag. As PROFESSOR FALKENHAUSEN, he uses a German accent.*)

RUDY. (*making the introductions*) Inspector Murzeau . . . Professor Falkenhausen . . .

MAX. Ach, what has happened? Am I disturbing you? (*RUDY nods towards MONIQUE, seated at the desk, crushed, her head in her hands.*) Lieber Gott! (*He crosses to her.*) Madame . . . good afternoon, madame. How are you feeling today?

MONIQUE. (*crying out*) Corbeau! Alive! And I saw her kill you right before my eyes! (*wagging of heads and sympathetic murmurs*)

MAX. (*to MONIQUE*) Now, now, madame! You

mustn't upset yourself! (*to RUDY*) She is not getting any better! (*to INSPECTOR*) Her paranoic schizophrenia is becoming dangerous! (*to SIMONE*) Give her an injection of phencyclidine, nurse!

Monique. (*crying out*) No! Don't touch me, you filthy beasts! (*She tries to escape . . . but SIMONE, who has doused a piece of cotton with chloroform, puts it over MONIQUE's nose. MONIQUE is overcome and falls on the sofa.*)

Inspector. (*to MAX*) Is there any chance of a cure, Professor? (*A small but, alas, despairing shrug from the 'PROFESSOR.' To RUDY:*) What do you intend to do, Monsieur Popesco?

Rudy. I don't know any more! I'm so upset! . . . But the problem I must resolve quickly is my wife's business affairs. I mean, from a financial viewpoint, I'm afraid she's no longer responsible for her actions. Inspector, I'm going to ask you, if you will, to put into your report everything that has happened here in your presence, which supports that contention.

Inspector. Certainly! . . . I'll even give you a copy of her deposition. Such delusions! (*SIMONE, head and shoulders back, crosses to the INSPECTOR.*)

Simone. Inspector, in light of these events, I must show you how madame amused herself this afternoon! (*And she takes out of her pocket all the checks that MONIQUE had signed and hands them to the INSPECTOR.*) . . . There's six hundred thousand francs here!

Inspector. Good God!

Simone. And, you will notice, these checks are made payable 'to bearer!' It's lucky she didn't walk around loose distributing them!

Rudy. It's frightening!

Max. Ach, yes! Delusions of grandeur!

INSPECTOR. Does Madame Popesco have any family in Switzerland?

RUDY. No, unfortunately. She's an orphan.

INSPECTOR. Then I advise you, monsieur, to block her bank account immediately.

RUDY. Thank you . . . I feared this might happen so I took the precaution of have a document drawn up, which permits her bank in Geneva to honor my signature. It needs only medical certification . . .

MAX. I am at your service, Monsieur Popesco.

RUDY. . . . and a statement from the Police.

INSPECTOR. Come to my office in the morning. I'll have a statement prepared.

RUDY. Thank you, gentlemen. (*He fights back his tears.*) Poor Monique! It's heartbreaking! I'll do everything to help her . . .

INSPECTOR. (*holding the checks*) Good man. What shall I do with these checks?

RUDY. Oh! Give them to me. I'll tear them up! (*He tears up the checks . . . that is, all but one.*) No, not this one! It's for you, Inspector . . . for the Policeman's Benevolent Fund. I'll countersign it tomorrow, then my signature will be valid . . . (*The INSPECTOR accepts the check. He is agreeably surprised by the amount.*)

INSPECTOR. Oh, it's too much!

RUDY. No, take it! It's nothing! I have a great deal of money . . . that is, my wife and I have! And if you could keep what happened here as quiet as possible . . . (*INSPECTOR starts to leave.*)

MONIQUE. (*gathering her strength*) No, no, Inspector! Don't go!

INSPECTOR. I'll drop in to see you again one of these days, madame.

MONIQUE. Please! I beg you . . .

INSPECTOR. Get well soon! (*He exits, accompanied by RUDY. Off-stage, he shouts to his men:*) Back to headquarters! (*SIMONE and MAX turn their smiles on MONIQUE. Her back stiffens. She is terrified.*)

MAX. Keep calm, madame . . . Don't move . . .

SIMONE. A little more chloroform?

MAX. This is going to be a . . . painful . . . evening for you, madame! (*The car doors slam, the motor starts up, the sirens wail . . . the POLICE are gone. RUDY returns and joins his two accomplices. They laugh, very pleased with themselves.*)

RUDY. Well, my darling wife, what do you say to that? Clever, wasn't it? Or are you still expecting your brother-in-law, Michel, to come to your rescue? Ah, here he is! (*He puts on MICHEL's glasses and becomes "MICHEL" again before our very eyes.*) 'Fresh as a daisy!'

SIMONE. (*putting her arms around RUDY's neck*) You were superb, baby! Superb!

MAX. (*to RUDY*) . . . What a brilliant idea to invent a brother you never had! When I returned and saw you disguised with that dejected 'out of prison look,' I could hardly contain myself. Congratulations!

RUDY. To you, too, my dear 'Corbeau.'

MAX. (*growling at MONIQUE*) Because of you I had to play a legal beagle! And I can't stand the crooked bastards!

SIMONE. Your palm-reading act was splendid, Max! Better than a gypsy! And when I fired, and you fell at my feet, dead . . . you gave me a scare!

RUDY. (*to SIMONE*) But you were splendid too, my puss! . . . You led my little Monique up to the garden path. You deserve something extra! (*He kisses her on the mouth.*)

SIMONE. Baby, you should have seen her face when she saw the letter from the prison that I planted . . .

RUDY. The letter we prepared.

MAX. I beg your pardon! The letter I prepared! The envelope was an exact copy of those used by the prison. And it was my handiwork! (*to MONIQUE*) You see, madame, I am in charge of props for this troupe . . . the gun and the blank bullets . . . the trick glass . . . (*He takes these items out of a small chest. Then, he busies himself with the telephone apparatus. RUDY picks up the trick glass and shows it to MONIQUE.*)

RUDY. Shall I show you, my darling, how I cut my hand? A trick glass and a capsule of hemoglobin. I crush the capsule and wham! (*He repeats the same action as in Act One, Scene One, while MONIQUE looks on frightened.*) And that stamped my two roles in your mind, didn't it? It made an indelible impression. The 'wicked' Rudy cut his hand and needed a dressing, while 'nice' MICHEL didn't have a scratch. Simple? (*SIMONE, who has slipped upstairs, comes down carrying two jackets and a large bag.*)

SIMONE. And the two jackets! (*She disappears into the kitchen.*)

RUDY. (*showing MONIQUE the two jackets*) Take care of the little things and the big things take care of themselves. I had two jackets made, one larger than the other, so Michel in the larger jacket would look thinner to you than Rudy. Simple? (*He puts the jackets in the bag.*) How is it coming along, Max?

MAX. One moment! It took me two hours to fix this telephone. I can't undo it in two seconds! (*He has unscrewed the base of the telephone and removed several coils which he pocketed. He replaced these coils with others. He is now winding up a very thin black wire, which he had cut from the telephone connection. Shouting:*) Simone! Where are you?

(*SIMONE returns with a suitcase with a trick bottom that conceals a tape recorder and a transmitter. She presses a button and a voice from the tape says:* "Madame Rudy Popesco? . . . Long distance calling. Bouches-du-Rhone . . . Are you ready? . . . Go ahead, Marseilles." *This is followed a few seconds later by a noise from an airport. RUDY picks up the microphone.*)

RUDY. 'Hello, my darling! This is Rudy. I'm at the airport. I'll be home in two hours!' . . . Isn't science wonderful? With this equipment, I was able to telephone you from the cellar! (*SIMONE and MAX put the props into the bag.*) But most of all I thank you for making the Inspector come here! We were delighted with your conversation! Yes! This room is bugged! We listened in from the empty house down the road! We heard the Inspector start to doubt your sanity! All we had to do was return and supply the finishing touches! (*The three villains laugh . . . a grating laugh.*) Now, honestly, isn't all this effort worth a fortune? I mean, your fortune? Answer me!

MONIQUE. (*weakly*) Yes . . . I believed it because it is possible for two brothers to look alike.

RUDY. (*sarcastically*) I'm pleased you appreciate our plan.

MONIQUE. But the perfect crime doesn't exist!

RUDY. Oh? You mean the famous 'grain of sand,' which jams the most perfect piece of criminal machinery? Oh! But you take us for beginners, don't you? Well, let me reassure you! We've already had four victories!

MONIQUE. Four?

RUDY. Yes! I may as well tell you! It will make you feel less alone! . . . You are my fifth wife! . . . This troupe made its first appearance in Berlin, where I met and married a rich Bavarian. The curtain went up! My wife thought her brother-in-law was coming out of prison! . . . Is the opening familiar? . . . When we demonstrated her error . . . she lost her sanity . . . and the the Police found her . . . dead from an overdose of sleeping pills.

SIMONE. His second wife was Peruvian. Same scenario. She was found . . . Madre de Dios . . . with every bone broken . . . at the bottom of a ravine.

MAX. . . . In London, his third wife . . . drowned in the Thames.

SIMONE. His fourth wife he met in Italy. A Neapolitan. She was as ugly as a louse . . .

MAX. But lousy with lira! . . . Crushed to death by a truck!

RUDY. Isn't life cruel! Four times I've been a widower! . . . Soon it will be five! And always I played these two roles . . . the ravenous wolf and the beaten dog. And always my dear wife, reduced to despair, asks herself: 'How can they look so alike and be so different?' And her faithful maid whispers: 'Why not use the dog to get rid of the wolf?' A fraudulent letter, drunken quarrels, a web of deceit climaxed by two mock murders! But there is also . . . and most important . . . a real Inspector, real depression, a fortune and certain death! (*a frightening silence*)

MONIQUE. Rudy . . . you want all my money, don't you?

RUDY. Yes.

MONIQUE. I'll give it to you.

RUDY. Thanks!
MONIQUE. . . . But let me . . . live!
RUDY. Do you think I'm that naive? (*dryly*) Max!
MAX. (*vilely*) What I suggest, madame, is 'suicide in the bath.' I'll leave a few books about . . .books on psychiatry, neurotic behaviour, depression. That should set the scene nicely, don't you think?
MONIQUE. (*crying out*) I'll stop you!
MAX. I doubt it!
MONIQUE. (*to RUDY*) You'll never get away with it!
RUDY. No? The Police will take pity on me, a poor, despondent husband whose wife went insane and committed suicide.
MONIQUE. But the others!
RUDY. Who is there to accuse me? My first four wives are . . . happily . . . silent.
MAX. And you, madame, will soon join them! (*They take a step towards her . . . She rises and says quietly:*)
MONIQUE. One moment! I have something to reveal, too . . . something I think will surprise you. I am not Monique. I am not rich and I am not a Swiss orphan! I assumed this identity in order to meet you, Rudy. Yes, I let myself be swept off my feet and into marriage. I became the woman you wanted me to be. And how I admired the way you played your dual role! But I did it because I wanted to stop you from killing for a fifth time! (*They start to move.*) Don't move! It's too late! My heart breaks for you! (*shouts*) Police! (*Suddenly, the INSPECTOR and the TWO POLICEMEN rush in, with their guns drawn. The trio is petrified.*) Thank you, Inspector! You helped me enormously in our last scene together. (*to the trio*) Everything was carefully planned. I knew you had bugged this room! Yes, these bugs are the cause of your downfall! Because of them,

you came back here . . . to fall into the hands of the Police! Inspector, may I have back my identity card? I can let them see it now! (*INSPECTOR gives her the card, with red, white and blue stripes and her photo, which she shows to the trio.*) Let me introduce myself: I am Georgette Feydeau . . . Interpol, Special Brigade, agent B-13. (*to INSPECTOR*) Mission accomplished! I turn these deadly 'comedians' over to you. May they laugh their heads off!

INSPECTOR. They will, Lieutenant! They will! (*On a gesture from the INSPECTOR, the TWO POLICEMEN take SIMONE and MAX away.*)

RUDY. (*crossing to GEORGETTE*) My congratulations, 'Lieutenant!'

GEORGETTE. Coming from you, I'm flattered.

RUDY. What courage to take on a bastard like me!

GEORGETTE. (*looking him straight in the eye*) Yes. But I got what I wanted . . . and a little bit more! (*While the INSPECTOR hurries RUDY away, her eyes follow him.*)

BLACKOUT

CURTAIN

PROPERTY LIST

a tray with coffee service for one:
    coffee pot, cup and saucer, teaspoon, 2 croissants, napkin
telephone
wristwatch (Louise)
letters, newspaper, magazines:
    one letter with large black seal on back of envelope
cigarillos
complete bar:
    bottles of whiskey, cognac, mineral water, etc., glasses
trick breakable glasses
checkbook
pen
stationery
notebook (Corbeau)
capsule of "blood"
bandage and dressing (Rudy)
suitcase (Rudy)
I.O.U.
wallet (Corbeau)
eyeglasses (Michel)
shabby suitcase (Michel)
cigarettes
cup of coffee
comb (Louise)
briefcase, with receipt inside (Corbeau)
bundle of franc notes
watch (Corbeau)
pair of scissors
roll of adhesive plaster
matches

cigarette lighter
ashtray
bottle of sleeping pills
ice bucket
smaller dressing (Rudy)
bottle of Beaujolais wine, uncorked
revolver (Rudy)
large sheets of writing paper (Michel)
legal papers (Corbeau)
bill for services rendered (Corbeau)
key in lock of kitchen door
3 messages (Policemen)
flashlight
bottle of smelling salts
wallet with identity card (Louise)
doctor's bag (Corbeau)
nurse's bag (Louise)
absorbent cotton
bottle of chloroform
small chest with gun, blank bullets, trick glass, capsule of "blood," telephone apparatus (Corbeau)
large bag with 2 jackets
suitcase with tape recorder and transmitter with microphone
2 guns (Policemen)
identity card (Monique)

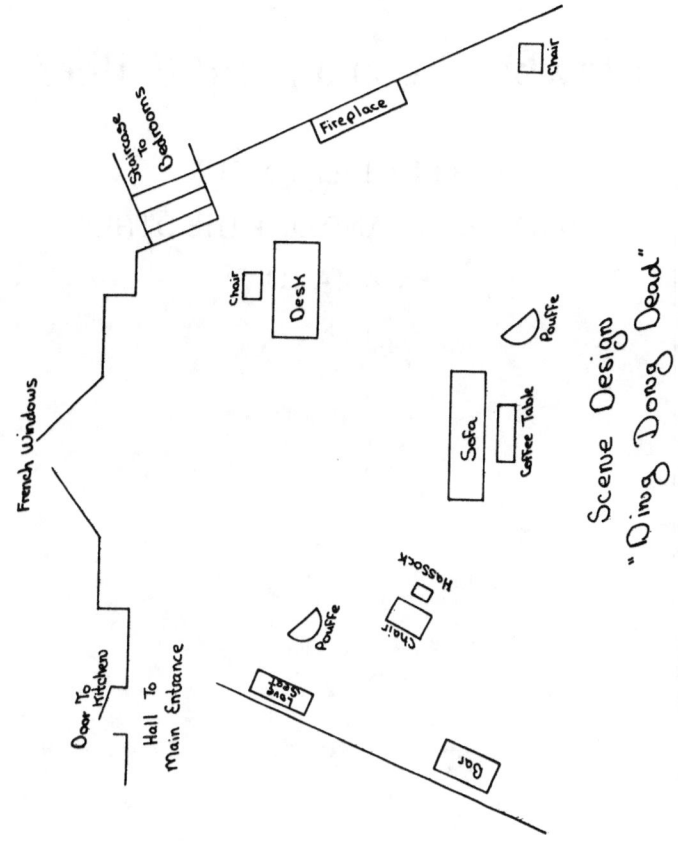

Also By
Mawby Green and Ed Feilbert

13 RUE DE L'AMOUR

IN ONE BED… AND OUT THE OTHER

PAJAMA TOPS

SAMUELFRENCH.COM

ABOUT THE ADAPTERS

The first collaboration of **Mawby Green** and **Ed Feilbert** was a dramatization of the Elizabeth Bowen novel THE HOUSE IN PARIS. The production introduced Ludmilla Pitoeff to American audiences, the late Mme. Pitoeff being George Bernard Shaw's French SAINT JOAN. Her leading man in HOUSE was a young actor, Yul Brynner.

Adaptations of two hit French farces by Jean de Letraz followed. IN ONE BED...AND OUT THE OTHER, heralded as a "laughter explosion," successfully toured the U.S., Canada, England and South Africa and is a tremendous audience-pleaser whenever and wherever it plays. PAJAMA TOPS is one of the longest running comedies ever produced, with five coast-to-coast U.S. tours, a six-year run in London, four tours in England, three in South Africa, two in Australia and is a perennial summer attraction in the British seaside resorts. The cable TV version, produced by Lorimar/Showtime, stars Robert Klein, Susan George and Pia Zadora.

Their 13 RUE DE L'AMOUR, based on a Feydeau farce, brought Leslie Caron and Louis Jourdan back together again for the first time since the film GIGI. Together the stars enjoyed a huge success in the Chicago production and 10-week Australian tour, but have not been free of commitments at the same time long enough for an open-end run, consequently, M. Jourdan appeared without Mme. Caron in both the London and Broadway productions. This adaptation of the uproarious Feydeau romp continues to delight in stock, amateur and regional theatres.

Leslie Caron has since enchanted summer theatre audiences in another Green/Feilbert adaptation, ONE FOR THE TANGO.

ABOUT THE FRENCH AUTHOR

Robert Thomas, born in 1930, is France's most successful playwright of thrillers. He made his debut in Paris as an actor in 1950, when the star he was understudying took ill 2 weeks after the opening night. Thomas continued as a journeyman actor, writing plays in his spare time, twelve of which never saw the light of day. But then, in 1960 came the famous PIEGE POUR UN HOMME SEUL (TRAP FOR A LONELY MAN) known throughout the United States as CATCH ME IF YOU CAN. Since then Thomas has had over ten plays produced in Paris and throughout the world, all of which have succeeded at the box-office. DING DONG DEAD (DOUBLE JEU) is his second thriller to be produced in the United States.

SAMUELFRENCH.COM

OTHER TITLES AVAILABLE FROM SAMUEL FRENCH

PAJAMA TOPS
Mawby Green and Ed Feilbert
From the French hit *Moumou* by Jean de Letraz

Farce / 4m, 3f / Interior

The plot is all fun. The husband is planning a business trip for philandering purposes; his wife secretly invites this same voluptuous girl to spend the weekend. The husband is trapped. Out of the blue an old friend appears, with hands aflutter, followed by a gendarme who delights in cherchez les femmes. There is also a devilish looking butler, a maid practising to be a cocotte, and some wildly artful dodging, all calculated to keep the audience laughing.

"An utterly mad spoof of the French bedroom farce."
– *The New York World Telegram & Sun*

"Prolonged laughter."
– *The New York Times*

"The best entertainment in London."
– *London Sunday Times*

SAMUELFRENCH.COM

OTHER TITLES AVAILABLE FROM SAMUEL FRENCH

THE DECORATOR
Donald Churchill

Comedy / 1m, 2f / Interior

Marcia returns to her flat to find it has not been painted as she arranged. A part time painter who is filling in for an ill colleague is just beginning the work when the wife of the man with whom Marcia is having an affair arrives to tell all to Marcia's husband. Marcia hires the painter a part time actor to impersonate her husband at the confrontation. Hilarity is piled upon hilarity as the painter, who takes his acting very seriously, portrays the absent husband. The wronged wife decides that the best revenge is to sleep with Marcia's husband, an ecstatic experience for them both. When Marcia learns that the painter/actor has slept with her rival, she demands the opportunity to show him what really good sex is.

"Irresistible."
– *London Daily Telegraph*

"This play will leave you rolling in the aisles....
I all but fell from my seat laughing."
– *London Star*

SAMUELFRENCH.COM

www.ingramcontent.com/pod-product-compliance
Lightning Source LLC
Chambersburg PA
CBHW070645300426
44111CB00013B/2275